GOD CALLING

✦ THE BARNES & NOBLE LIBRARY OF ESSENTIAL READING ✦

GOD CALLING
A Devotional Diary

EDITED AND WITH AN INTRODUCTION BY
A. J. RUSSELL

BARNES & NOBLE

NEW YORK

THE BARNES & NOBLE
LIBRARY OF ESSENTIAL READING

Originally published in 1934

This 2007 edition published by Barnes & Noble, Inc.

ISBN-13: 978-0-7607-9689-4
ISBN-10: 0-7607-9689-0

Printed and bound in the United States of America

1 3 5 7 9 10 8 6 4 2

CONTENTS

THE TWO LISTENERS

I DID NOT WRITE THIS BOOK. I WISH I HAD DONE SO.

Had I written it I should have been immeasurably proud. Too proud for spiritual health.

My simple task has been to prepare it for publication and to present it to the public. But that has not really been a task—only a privilege; an undeserved honor.

There is a legend that the praise for building the Cathedral of St. Sofia was not given to the Emperor Constantine but to Euphrasia, a poor widow who drew from her mattress "a wisp of straw and gave it to the oxen" that drew the marble from the ships. That was all; she did nothing more.

Not one woman but two have written this book; and they seek no praise. They elected to remain anonymous and to be called "Two Listeners." But the claim which they make is an astonishing one, that their message has been given to them, today, here in England, by the living Christ himself.

Having read their book, I believed them.

I do not, of course, believe that he whispered to them all that he intends to say to this generation. But I am confident that he opened their eyes to many things which they and this generation greatly need to know.

I do not believe in the verbal inspiration of this or any book. But I do believe that these two women have been led and that much of what is written is very clear leading indeed.

I have found these messages a spiritual stimulus. But that statement is as inadequate as to say that I like England. None could have written this book unless he or she was a Christian and in touch with the Living Founder of Christianity.

We hear much of the decline of the drama. Think of this piece of real drama, of our own times. Again, as so often before, "He was in the world and the world knew Him not."

Two poor, brave women were courageously fighting against sickness and penury. They were facing a hopeless future and one of them even longed to be quit of this hard world for good. And then he spoke. And spoke again!

Day after day he comes and cheers them. And though they still have their sorrows they have joy and a new courage. For he inspires them with his promises for their future when his loving purpose shall be revealed; and he gently rallies them on their unbelief, as he did their forlorn predecessors during that walk to Emmaus.

Open this book at any page and taste its beauty. Dwell lovingly on its tender phrases. Let its wonderful quality sink deep into your spirit.

Have you lost faith? Meditate on any one of these tiny sections and it will come again to you as that of a little child. You may not see him standing by your side with his ready smile of confident encouragement; but you will know that he is there, as he always is, and that he still expects great things of you, and is ever ready to help you to achieve them.

If winter comes—are you afraid of poverty? Turn again to these pages and you will find the law of supply—Give and it shall be given you. Give your love, your time, your sympathy, yourself; give all that you have under his direct guidance to all who are needy; give both to the deserving and the undeserving.

Has health gone? Are you no better though you have prayed long and often? Here again you will find the incense of healing; you will understand why he will not remove the gold from the crucible until all the dross has gone, and you are taking the glorious shape of your true self, which his eye alone has foreseen.

You cannot eat honey all the day. Nor can you read this book through at a sitting. But you can read it every day, and several times a day.

It can be turned to in the heat of a sudden crisis, and when you put it down you will find yourself calm and at peace within.

You can open its pages when the birds are singing in the sunshine; and as you read, the song of the birds will be echoed in your spirit, for you too will be carolling your love to our creator-redeemer.

Put this book of "Daily Power" in your pocket, in your handbag, on the table by your bedside. Give a copy of it to your friends.

Inhale its spirit continually and live your life in its intimacy with the master.

Through this message, which came to two lonely women, you will find that you are no longer one and alone, but two and united with the great companion and guide, who is the same yesterday, today, and forever.

A. J. RUSSELL

If Two Agree

If two of you shall agree on earth as touching anything that they shall ask, it shall be done for them of my Father which is in heaven.

For where two or three are gathered together in my name there am I in the midst of them.

THE VOICE DIVINE

By

One of the "Two Listeners"

IN THE AUTUMN OF 1932, I WAS SITTING IN THE LOUNGE OF AN HOTEL when a visitor, quite unknown, crossed over and, handing me a copy of *For Sinners Only*, asked if I had read it. I answered "No," and she left it with me.

On returning home, I bought a copy for myself.

I was curiously affected by the book and felt that I wanted all my friends to read it immediately, and actually made out a list of over a hundred people to whom I should have liked to have sent it. Not being rich, this desire had to be content with two copies, which I lent to various people, on whom it seemed to make little effect.

A few months later I read it again. It was then that there came a persistent desire to try to see whether I could get guidance such as A. J. Russell reported, through sharing a quiet time with the friend with whom I was then living. She was a deeply spiritual woman with unwavering faith in the goodness of God and a devout believer in prayer, although her life had not been an easy one.

I was rather skeptical, but, as she agreed, we sat down, pencils and paper in hand and waited. This was in December 1932.

My results were entirely negative. Portions of texts came and went, then my mind wandered to ordinary topics. I brought it back again and again, but with no success. To this day, I cannot get guidance in this way alone.

But with my friend a very wonderful thing happened. From the first, beautiful messages were given to her by our Lord himself, and every day from then these messages have never failed us.

We felt all unworthy and overwhelmed by the wonder of it, and could hardly realize that *we* were being taught, trained, and encouraged day by day by him personally, when millions of souls, far worthier, had to be content with guidance from the Bible, sermons, their churches, books, and other sources.

Certainly we were not in any way psychic or advanced in spiritual growth, but just very ordinary human beings, who had had more suffering and worry than the majority and who had known tragedy after tragedy.

The tender understanding of some of Our Lord's messages was at times almost heartbreaking: but his loving reproofs would leave no hurt.

Always, and this daily, he insisted that we should be channels of love, joy, and laughter in his broken world. This was the Man of Sorrows in a new aspect.

We, or rather I, found this command very difficult to obey, although to others it might have been simple. To laugh, to cheer others, to be always joyful when days were pain-racked, nights tortured by chronic insomnia, when poverty and almost insupportable worry were our daily portion, when prayer went unanswered and God's face was veiled and fresh calamities came upon us?

Still came this insistent command to love and laugh and be joy-bringers to the lives we contacted.

Disheartened, one of us would gladly have ceased the struggle and passed on to another and happier life.

But he encouraged us daily, saying that he would not break the instruments that he intended to use, that he would not leave the metal in the crucible longer than was necessary for the burning away of the dross. Continually he exhorted us not to lose heart, and spoke of the joy that the future held for us.

Totally unexpected interpretations of his own words were given.

An adverse verdict on seeing visions of himself, which we had hitherto thought granted only to the saintliest and, most strongly stressed of all, the immense power given to *two* souls praying together in close union and at one in their desire to love and serve him. As others have proved, "such a union may, in God's hands, accomplish such great things that there certainly will be inimical forces whose purpose it is to mar the friendship." And so we found it.

Some of the messages are of surprising beauty. The majestic language of December 2nd, the inevitability of suffering in the Christian life of November 23rd, and the explanation of the practical working of the law of supply of December 5th are examples of this.

Others may appear disjointed. This is because personal references and repetition have had to be deleted.

So to us this book, which we believe has been guided by our Lord himself, is no ordinary book.

It is published, after much prayer, to prove that a living Christ speaks today, plans and guides the humblest, that no detail is too insignificant for his attention, that he reveals himself now as ever as a Humble Servant and majestic Creator.

JANUARY

BETWEEN THE YEARS   JANUARY 1

Our Lord and our God. We joy in Thee. Without Thy help we could
not face unafraid the year before us.

I stand between the years. The light of my presence is flung across
the year to come—the radiance of the Sun of righteousness.
Backward, over the past year, is my shadow thrown, hiding trouble
and sorrow and disappointment.

Dwell not on the past—only on the present. Only use the past
as the trees use my Sunlight to absorb it, to make from it in after
days the warming fire-rays. So store only the blessings from me, the
light of the world. Encourage yourselves by the thought of these.

Bury every fear of the future, of poverty for those dear to you, of
suffering, of loss. Bury all thought of unkindness and bitterness, all
your dislikes, your resentments, your sense of failure, your disappointment in others and in yourselves, your gloom, your despondency,
and let us leave them all, buried, and go forward to a new and
risen life.

Remember that you must not see as the world sees. I hold the
year in my hands—in trust for you. But I shall guide you one day at
a time.

Leave the rest with me. You must not anticipate the gift by fears
or thoughts of the days ahead.

And for each day I shall supply the wisdom and the strength.

ARM OF LOVE   JANUARY 2

You are to help to save others. Never let one day pass when you have
not reached out an arm of love to someone outside your home—a
note, a letter, a visit, help in some way.

Be full of joy. Joy saves. Joy cures. Joy in me. In every ray of sunlight, every smile, every act of kindness, or love, every trifling
service—joy.

Each day do something to lift another soul out of the sea of sin, or
disease or doubt into which man has fallen. I still walk today by the
lakeside and call my disciples to follow me and to become fishers
of men.

The helping hand is needed that raises the helpless to courage, to
struggle, to faith, to health. Love and laugh. Love and laughter are
the beckoners to faith and courage and success. Trust on, love on,
joy on.

Refuse to be downcast. Refuse to be checked in your upward
climb. Love and laugh. I am with you. I bear your burdens. Cast your
burden upon me and I will sustain thee. And then in very lightheart-
edness you turn and help another with the burden that is pressing
too heavily upon him or her.

How many burdens can you lighten this year? How many hearts
can you cheer? How many souls can you help?

And in giving you gain: "Good measure, pressed down and running over." I your Lord have said it.

THE WAY WILL OPEN   JANUARY 3

They that wait upon the Lord shall renew their strength. (Isa. xl. 31)

You must be renewed, remade. Christ, Christ, Christ. Everything must
rest on me. Force is born of rest. Only love is a conquering force. Be
not afraid, I will help you.

Be channels both of you. My Spirit shall flow through and my
Spirit shall, in flowing through, sweep away all the bitter past.

Take heart, God loves, God helps, God fights, God wins. You
shall see. You shall know. The way will open. All my love has ever

planned, all my love has ever thought, you shall see each day unfold. Only be taught. Just be a child. A child never questions plans. It accepts gladly.

Do Not Plan   JANUARY 4

Shew us Thy way, O Lord, and let us walk in Thy paths. Lead us in Thy truth and teach us.

All is well. Wonderful things are happening. Do not limit God at all. He cares and provides.

Uproot self—the channel-blocker. Do not plan ahead, the way will unfold step by step. Leave tomorrow's burden. Christ is the great Burden-bearer. You cannot bear his load and he only expects you to carry a little day-share.

Hoard Nothing   JANUARY 5

Love me and do my will. No evil shall befall you. Take no thought for tomorrow. Rest in my presence brings peace. God will help you. Desire brings fulfillment. Peace like a quiet flowing river cleanses, sweeps all irritants away.

You shall be taught, continue these prayer-times, even if they seem fruitless. The devil will try by any means to stop them. Heed him not. He will say evil spirits may enter in. Heed him not.

Rest your nerves. Tired nerves are a reflection on, not of, God's power. Hope all the time.

Do not be afraid of poverty. Let money flow freely. I will let it flow in but you must let it flow out. I never send money to stagnate—only to those who pass it on. Keep nothing for yourself. Hoard nothing. Only have what you need and use. This is my law of discipleship.

Sharp and Ready   JANUARY 6

Guide me, O Thou great Jehovah,
Pilgrim through this foreign land.
I am weak but Thou art mighty,
Guide me with Thy powerful hand.

You must pray. The way will open. God cares and his plans unfold. Just love and wait.

Love is the key. No door is too difficult for it to open.

What cause have you to fear? Has he not cared for and protected you? Hope on. Hope gladly. Hope with certainty. Be calm, calm in my power.

Never neglect these times, pray and read your Bible and train and discipline yourself. That is your work—mine to use you. But my instruments must be sharp and ready. Then I use them.

Discipline and perfect yourselves at all costs. Do this for soon every fleeting thought will be answered, every wish gratified, every deed used. It is a fearful power, a mighty power. Oh! Be careful that you ask nothing amiss—nothing that is not according to my Spirit.

All thoughts harmful must be turned out. Miracle-working power can become witchery in wrong hands. See how necessary I have made the purity and goodness of your own lives to you. That is why. Soon, very soon, you shall ask and at once it will come. Welcome the training. Without it I dare not give you this power. It would do harm.

Do not worry about others' lives. That will all come right. You must perfect yourselves first in my strength.

THE SECRET PEARL   JANUARY 7

Look upon us with Thy favor, O Lord, while we behold "the land that is very far off" and yet so near to the seeing eye and the listening ear.

Wait. Wonders are unfolding. Tremble with awe. No man can stand upon the threshold of Eternity unshaken. I give unto you eternal life. A free gift, a wonderful gift—the life of the Ages.

Silently comes the kingdom. No man can judge when It enters the heart of man, only in results. Listen quietly. Sometimes you may get no message. Meet thus all the same. You will absorb an atmosphere.

Cultivate silence. "God speaks in silences." A silence, a soft wind. Each can be a message to convey my meaning to the heart, though by no voice, or even word.

Each word or thought of yours can be like a pearl that you drop into the secret place of another heart, and in some hour of need, lo! The recipient finds the treasure and realizes for the first time its value.

•   •   •   •

Do not be too ready to *do*, just *be*. I said, "*Be* ye therefore perfect" not "do" perfect things. Try and grasp this. Individual efforts avail nothing. It is only the work of the Universal Spirit—my Spirit, that counts.

Dwell in thought on this, more and more, saints have taken a lifetime to grasp it.

LOVE BANGS THE DOOR   JANUARY 8

Life with me is not immunity *from* difficulties, but peace *in* difficulties. My guidance is often by *shut* doors. Love bangs as well as opens.

Joy is the result of faithful trusting acceptance of my will, when It seems *not* joyous.

St. Paul, my servant, learnt this lesson of the banged doors when he said "our light affliction, which is but for a moment, worketh for us a far more exceeding and eternal weight of glory." Expect rebuffs until this is learned—it is the only way.

Joy is the daughter of calm.

NO STRAIN   JANUARY 9

Be calm, no matter what may befall you. Rest in me. Be patient, and let patience have her perfect work. Never think things overwhelming. How can you be overwhelmed when I am with you?

Do not feel the strain of life. There is no strain for my children. Do you not see I am a master Instrument-maker? Have I not fashioned each part? Do I not know just what it can bear without a strain? Would I, the maker of so delicate an instrument, ask of it anything that could destroy or strain?

No! The strain is only when you are serving another master, the world, fame, the good opinion of men—or carrying two days' burden on the one day.

Remember that it must not be.

INFLUENCE   JANUARY 10

When you come to me, and I give you that eternal life I give to all who believe in me, it alters your whole existence, the words you speak, the influences you have.

These are all eternal. They *must* be. They spring from the life within you, my life, eternal life, so that they too live forever. Now, you see how vast, how stupendous, is the work of any soul that has eternal life. The words, the influence, go on down the ages forever.

You must ponder on these truths I give you. They are not surface facts, but the secrets of my kingdom, the hidden pearls of rare price.

Meditate upon them. Work at them in your minds and hearts.

THE ACHE OF LOVE   JANUARY 11

Cry unto me, and I will hear you and bless you. Use my unlimited stores for your needs and those of others. Seek my wonderful truths and you *shall* find.

There may come times when you sit in silence, when it seems as if you were left alone. Then, I command—*command*—you to remember I have spoken to you, as I spoke at Emmaus.

But there was the time in the upper room, after my ascension, when my disciples had to comfort themselves by saying, "Did he not speak to us by the way?"

You will have the consciousness of my presence when you hear no voice. Abide in that presence. "I am the light of the world," but sometimes in tender pity, I withhold too glaring a light, lest, in its dazzling brightness, you should miss your daily path and work.

Not until heaven is reached, do souls sit and drink in the ecstasy of God's revelation to his own. At the moment you are pilgrims and need only your daily marching orders, and strength and guidance for the day.

Oh! Listen to my voice, eagerly, joyfully. Never crowd it out. I have no rival claimants and if men seek the babble of the world, then I withdraw.

Life has hurt you. Only scarred lives can really save.

•   •   •   •

You cannot escape the discipline. It is the hallmark of discipleship. My children, trust me always. Never rebel.

The trust given to me today, takes away the ache of rejection of my love, that I suffered on earth, and have suffered through the ages. "I died for you, my children, and could ye treat me so?"

THANKS FOR TRIALS   JANUARY 12

You must say "Thank You" for everything, even seeming trials and worries.

Joy is the whole being's attitude of "Thank You" to me. Be glad. Rejoice. A father loves to see his children happy.

I am revealing so much to you. Pass it on. Each truth is a jewel. Some poor spirit-impoverished friend will be glad of it. Drop one here and there.

Seek to find a heart-home for each truth I have imparted to you. More truths will flow in. Use *all* I give you. Help others. I ache to find a way into each life and heart, for all to cry expectantly, "Even so, come Lord Jesus."

FRIENDS UNSEEN   JANUARY 13

Never despair, never despond. Be just a channel of helpfulness for others.

Have more sympathy. Feel more tenderness towards others. Your lives shall not be all care. *Gold* does not *stay* in the crucible—*only* until it is refined. Already I hear the music and the marching of the unseen host, rejoicing at your victory.

No follower of mine would ever err or fall, if once the veil were withdrawn which prevents him seeing how these slips delight the evil spirits, and the pain and disappointment of those who long for him to conquer in my strength and name, and the ecstasy of rejoicing when victory is won.

My strength is *the same* as that in which I conquered Satan in the Wilderness—depression and sorrow in the Garden, and even Death on Calvary.

Think of that.

MIGHTY AND MARVELOUS   JANUARY 14

Glad indeed are the souls with whom I walk. Walking with me is security. The coming of my Spirit into a life, and Its working are imperceptible, but the result is mighty.

Learn of me. Kill the self. Every blow to self is used to shape the real, eternal, imperishable you.

Be very candid and rigorous with yourselves. "Did *self* prompt that?" and if it did, oust it at all costs.

When I died on the cross, I died embodying all the human self. Once that was crucified, I could conquer even death.

When I bore your sins in my own body on the tree I bore the self-human nature of the world. As you too kill self, you gain the overwhelming power I released for a weary world, and you too will be victorious.

It is not life and its difficulties you have to conquer, only the self in you. As I said to my disciples, "I have many things to say to you but you cannot bear them now." You could not understand them. But as you go on obeying me and walking with me, and listening to me, you will, and then you will see how glorious, how marvelous my revelations are, and my teachings.

RELAX   JANUARY 15

Relax, do not get tense, have no fear. All is for the best. How can you fear change when your life is hid with me in God, who changeth not—and I am the same yesterday, today, and forever.

You must learn poise, soul-balance and poise, in a vacillating, changing world.

Claim my power. The same power with which I cast out devils is yours today. Use it. If not, I withdraw it. Use it ceaselessly.

You cannot ask too much. Never think you are too busy. As long as you get back to me and replenish after each task no work can be too much. My joy I give you. Live in it. Bathe your Spirit in it. Reflect it.

FRIEND IN DRUDGERY   JANUARY 16

It is the daily strivings that count, not the momentary heights. The obeying of my will day in, day out, in the wilderness plains, rather than the occasional Mount of Transfiguration.

Perseverance is nowhere needed so much as in the religious life. The drudgery of the kingdom it is that secures my intimate friendship. I am the Lord of little things, the divine control of little happenings.

Nothing in the day is too small to be a part of my scheme. The little stones in a mosaic play a big part.

Joy in me. Joy is the God-given cement that secures the harmony and beauty of my mosaic.

GOD'S RUSH TO GIVE   JANUARY 17

Silence. Be silent before me. Seek to *know,* and then to *do* my will in *all* things.

Abide in my love. An atmosphere of loving understanding to all men. This is *your* part to carry out, and then *I* surround you with a protective screen that keeps all evil from you. It is fashioned by your own attitude of mind, words, and deeds towards others.

I want to give you all things, good measure, pressed down and running over. Be quick to learn. You know little yet of the divine Impatience which longs to rush to give. Does one worrying thought enter your mind, one impatient thought? Fight it at once.

Love and Trust are the solvents for the worry and cares and frets of a life. Apply them *at once.* You are channels, and though the channel may not be altogether blocked, fret and impatience and worry corrode, and in time would become beyond your help.

Persevere, oh! Persevere. Never lose heart. All is well.

FAITH—WORKS   JANUARY 18

Pray daily for faith. It is my gift.

It is your only requisite for the accomplishment of mighty deeds. Certainly you have to work, you have to pray, but upon faith alone depends the answer to your prayers—your works.

I give it you in response to your prayer, because it is the necessary weapon for you to possess for the dispersion of evil—the overcoming of all adverse conditions, and the accomplishment of all good in your lives, and then you having faith, give it back to me. It is the envelope in which every request to me should be placed.

And yet "faith without works is dead." So you need works, too, to feed your faith in me. As you seek to do, you feel your helplessness. You then turn to me. In knowing me, your faith grows—and that faith is all you need for my power to work.

LOVE ANTICIPATES   JANUARY 19

Lord, I will seek Thee.

None ever sought me in vain. I wait, wait with a hungry longing to be called upon; and I, who have already seen your hearts' needs before you cried upon me, before perhaps, you were conscious of those needs yourself, I am already preparing the answer.

It is like a mother, who is setting aside suitable gifts for her daughter's wedding, before love even has come into the daughter's life.

The *Anticipatory love* of God is a thing mortals seldom realize. Dwell on this thought. Dismiss from your minds the thought of a grudging God, who had to be petitioned with sighs and tears and much speaking before reluctantly he loosed the desired treasures. Man's thoughts of me need revolutionizing.

Try and see a mother preparing birthday or Christmas delights for her child—the while her mother-heart sings: "Will she not love that? How she will love this!" and anticipates the rapture of her child, her own heart full of the tenderest joy. Where did the mother learn all this preparation—joy? From me—a faint echo this of my preparation—joy.

Try to see this as plans unfold of my preparing. It means much to me to be understood, and the understanding of me will bring great joy to you.

AT ONE WITH GOD   JANUARY 20

One with me. I and my Father are one. One with the Lord of the whole universe!

Could human aspiration reach higher? Could man's demands transcend this? One with me.

If you realize your high privilege, you have only to think and immediately the object of your thought is called into being. Indeed, well may I have said, "Set your affections on things above, not on things of the earth."

To dwell in thought on the material, when once you live in me—is to call it into being. So you must be careful only to think of and desire that which will help, not hinder, your spiritual growth. The same law operates too on the spiritual plane.

Think *love,* and love surrounds you, and all about whom you think. Think thoughts of *ill-will* and ill surrounds you, and those about whom you think. Think health—health comes. The physical reflects the mental and spiritual.

A CROWDED DAY   JANUARY 21

Believe that I am with you, and controlling all. When my Word has gone forth, *all* are powerless against it.

Be calm. Never fear. You have much to learn. Go on until you can take the most crowded day with a song. "Sing unto the Lord." The finest accompaniment to a Song of praise to me is a very crowded day. Let love be the motif running through all.

Be glad all the time. Rejoice exceedingly. Joy in me. Rest in me. Never be afraid. Pray more. Do not get worried. I am thy helper. "Underneath are the Everlasting Arms." You cannot get below that. Rest in them, as a tired child rests.

GREY DAYS   JANUARY 22

Be not afraid. I am your God, your Deliverer. From all evil, I will deliver you. Trust me. Fear not.

Never forget your "Thank You." Do you not see it is a lesson? You *must* say "Thank You" on the greyest days. You *must* do it. All cannot be light unless you do. There is grey-day practice. It is absolutely necessary.

My death upon the cross was not only necessary to save a world, it was necessary, if only to train my disciples. It was all a part of their training: my entering Jerusalem in triumph; my washing the disciples' feet; my sorrow-time in Gethsemane; my being despised, judged, crucified, buried. Every step was necessary to their development— and so with you.

If a grey day is not one of thankfulness, the lesson has to be repeated until it is. Not to everyone is it so. But only to those who ask to serve me well, and to do much for me. A great work requires a great and careful training.

How Power Comes   January 23

Lord, Thou art our Refuge. Our God, in Thee do we trust. O master come and talk with us.

All power is given unto me. It is mine to give, mine to withhold, *but* even I have to acknowledge that I cannot withhold it from the soul that dwells near me, because it is then not a gift, but passes insensibly from me to my disciples.

It is breathed in by the soul who lives in my presence.

Learn to shut yourself away in my presence—and then, without speaking, you have those things you desire of me, strength—power— joy—Riches.

Your Great Reward   January 24

You pray for faith, and you are told to do so. But I make provision in the house of my Abiding for those who turn towards me and yet have weak knees and hearts that faint. Be not afraid. I am your God. Your great Reward. Yours to look up and say "All is well."

I am your guide. Do not want to see the road ahead. Go just one step at a time. I very rarely grant the long vista to my disciples, especially in personal affairs, for one step at a time is the best way to cultivate faith.

You are in uncharted waters. But the Lord of all seas is with you, the controller of all storms is with you. Sing with joy. You follow the Lord of limitations, as well as the God in whose service is perfect freedom.

He, the God of the universe, confined himself within the narrow limits of a baby-form and, in growing boyhood, and young manhood, submitted to your human limitations, and you have to learn that your vision and power, boundless as far as spiritual things are concerned, must in temporal affairs submit to limitations too.

But I am with you. It was when the disciples gave up effort after a night of fruitless fishing, that I came, and the nets broke with the overabundance of supply.

WAY OF HAPPINESS   JANUARY 25

Complete surrender of every moment to God is the *foundation* of happiness, the *superstructure* is the joy of Communion with him. And that is, for each, the place, the mansion, I went to prepare for you.

My followers have misunderstood that, and looked too often upon that promise as referring only to an After-life, and too often—far too often—upon this life as a something to be struggled through, in order to get the reward and the joy of the next.

Seek to carry out all I say, and such understanding, insight, vision and joy will be yours as shall pass indeed all understanding. The plans of God are very wonderful—beyond your highest hopes.

Cling to thoughts of protection, safety, guidance.

KEEP CALM   JANUARY 26

Keep your Spirit-life calm and unruffled. Nothing else matters. Leave all to me. This is your great task, to get calm in my presence, not to let one ruffled feeling stay for one moment. Years of blessing may be checked in one moment by that.

No matter *who* frets you or what, yours is the task to stop all else until absolute calm comes. Any block means my power diverted into other channels.

Pour forth—pour forth—pour forth—I cannot bless a life that does not act as a channel. My Spirit brooks no stagnation, not even rest. Its power must flow on. Pass on everything, every blessing. Abide in me.

See how many you can bless each day. Dwell much in my presence.

HEIGHT OF THE STORM   JANUARY 27

Lord, to whom shall we go? Thou hast the words of eternal life.

(John vi. 68)

I am with you both. Go forward unafraid. Health and strength, peace and happiness and joy—they are all my gifts. Yours for the asking.

In the spiritual (as in the material) world there is no empty space, and as self, and fears and worries depart out of your lives, it follows that the things of the Spirit, that you crave so, rush in to take their places. All things are yours, and ye are Christ's, and Christ is God's. What a wonderful cycle, because ye are God's.

Be not afraid. Fear not. It is to the drowning man the rescuer comes. To the brave swimmer who can fare well alone he comes not. And no rush of joy *can* be like that of a man towards his rescuer.

It is a part of my method to wait till the storm is at its full violence. So did I with my disciples on the Lake. I could have bidden the first angry wave be calm, the first gust of wind be still, but what a lesson unlearned? What a sense of tender nearness of refuge and safety would have been lost.

Remember this—my disciples thought that in sleep I had forgotten them. Remember how mistaken they were. Gain strength and confidence and joyful dependence and anticipation from that.

Never fear. Joy is yours, and the radiant joy of the rescued shall be yours.

Low Ambitions   January 28

Fear not. Do not fear to be busy. You are the servant of all. "He that would be the greatest among you, let him be the servant of all."

Service is the word of my disciples. I served indeed, the humblest, the lowliest. I was at their command. My highest powers were at their service.

Be used. Be used by all, by the lowest, the smallest. How best you can serve? Let that be your daily seeking, not how best can you be served.

Truly man's thoughts are not God's thoughts, nor man's ways, God's ways. When you seek to follow me in all, it frequently means a complete reversion of the way of the world you have hitherto followed. But it is a reversion that leads to boundless happiness and peace.

Look around you, read what is being written. What do you find? Do the aims and ambitions that man strives for bring peace, or the world's awards bring heart-rest and happiness? No! Indeed, man is at war with man. Those whom the world has most rewarded, with name, fame, honor, wealth, are weary and disappointed.

And yet, to the listening ear, above the jangle of the world's discordant cries, there echoes down the 1900 years my message, "Come unto me all ye that are weary and heavy laden and I will give you rest."

And the weary and disappointed who listen and turn to me find indeed that rest. Joy of the weary I am, music to the heart I am, health to the sick, wealth to the poor, food to the hungry, home to the wanderer, rapture to the jaded, love to the lonely.

There is not *one* want of the soul, that I do not supply for the asking, and to you too, I long to be all.

I CLEAR THE PATH   JANUARY 29

Wait on the Lord.   (Psalm xxvii. 14)

I am thy shield. Have no fear. You must know that "All is well." I will never let anyone do to you both, other than my will for you.

I can see the future. I can read men's hearts. I know better than you what you need. Trust me absolutely. You are not at the mercy of Fate, or buffeted about by others. You are being led in a very definite way, and others, who do not serve your purpose, are being moved out of your path by me.

Never fear, whatever may happen. You are both being led. Do not try to plan. I have planned. You are the builder, *not* the Architect.

Go very quietly, very gently. All is for the very best for you.

Trust me for all. Your very extremity will ensure my activity for you. And having your foundation on the rock—Christ, faith in him, and "being rooted and grounded in him," and having belief in my divinity as your cornerstone, it is yours to build, knowing all is well.

Literally, you have to depend on me for everything—everything. It was out of the depths that David cried unto me, and I heard his voice. All is well.

THE SOUL AT WAR   JANUARY 30

No evil can befall you, if I am with you. "Ill that he blesses is our good." Every time of being laid aside is a time of retreat into the quiet place with me. Never fear but in that place you shall find restoration and power and joy and healing.

Plan both of your retreat days now and then—days when you live apart with me, and arise rested and refreshed—physically, mentally, and spiritually, to carry on the work I have given to you. I will never give you a load greater than you can bear.

Love, joy, peace, welcome these. Let no personal feelings, no thoughts of self banish these. Singly, they are miracle-producing in a life, but together, they can command all that is needed on the physical, mental, and spiritual planes.

It is in these wonder-realm attributes, all success lies. You have to see your inner lives are all they should be, and then the work is accomplished. Not in rushing and striving on the material plane, but on the battlefield of the soul are these things won.

SUFFERING REDEEMS   JANUARY 31

All sacrifice and all suffering is redemptive: to teach the individual or to be used to raise and help others.

Nothing is by chance.

Divine mind and its wonder working, is beyond your finite mind to understand.

No detail is forgotten in my Plans, already perfect.

FEBRUARY

ANOTHER START   FEBRUARY 1

Take courage. Do not fear. Start a new life tomorrow. Put the old mistakes away, and start anew. I give you a fresh start. Be not burdened. Be not anxious. If my forgiveness were for the righteous only, and those who had not sinned, where would be its need?

Remember as I said to Mary of old, "To whom much is forgiven, the same loveth much."

Why do you fret and worry so? I wait to give you all that is lovely, but your lives are soiled with worry and fret. You would crush my treasures. I can only bless glad, thankful hearts.

You *must* be glad and joyful.

PRACTICE LOVE   FEBRUARY 2

Watch over and protect us.

Want of love will block the way. You *must* love all. Those that fret you and those who do not.

Practice love. It is a great lesson, and you have a great teacher. You *must* love, how otherwise can you dwell in me, where nothing unloving can come? Practice this and I will bless you exceedingly, above all you cannot only ask, but imagine.

No limit to my power. Do all you can and leave to me the rest. Peace will come and trust. Fear not, I am your advocate, your mediator.

17

IF MEN OPPOSE   FEBRUARY 3

Only believe. The Walls of Jericho fell down. Was it axes or human implements that brought them down? Rather the Songs of praise of the people and my thought carried out in action.

All walls shall fall before you, too. There is no earth-power. It falls like a house of paper, at my miracle-working touch. Your faith and my power—the only two essentials. Nothing else is needed.

So, if man's petty opposition still holds good it is only because I choose to let it stand between you and what would be a mistake for you. If not—a word—a thought—from me, and it is gone. The hearts of kings are in my rule and governance. All men can be moved at my wish.

Rest in this certainty. Rely on me.

DROP YOUR CRUTCH   FEBRUARY 4

Just go step by step. My will shall be revealed as you go. You will never cease to be thankful for this time when you felt at peace and trustful, and yet had no human security.

That is the time of the True learning of trust in me. "When thy father and mother forsake thee, then the Lord will take thee up." This is a literal dependence on me.

When human support or material help of any kind is removed, then my power can become operative. I cannot teach a man to walk who is trusting to a crutch. Away with your crutch, and my power shall so invigorate you that you shall indeed walk on to victory. Never limit my power. It is limitless.

YOU SHALL KNOW   FEBRUARY 5

Walk with me. I will teach you. Listen to me and I will speak. Continue to meet me, in spite of all opposition and every obstacle, in spite of days when you may hear no voice, and there may come no intimate heart-to-heart telling.

As you persist in this, and make a life-habit of it, in many marvelous ways I will reveal my will to you. You shall have more sure knowing of both the present and the future. But that will be only the reward of the regular coming to meet me.

Life is a school. There are many teachers. Not to everyone do I come personally. Believe literally that the problems and difficulties of your lives can be explained by me more clearly and effectually than by any other.

GOD'S LONGING   FEBRUARY 6

To the listening ear I speak, to the waiting heart I come. Sometimes, I may not speak. I may ask you merely to wait in my presence, to know that I am with you.

Think of the multitudes, who thronged me, when I was on earth, all eager for something. Eager to be healed, or taught, or fed.

Think as I supplied their many wants, and granted their manifold requests, what it meant to me, to find amid the crowd, some one or two, who followed me just to be near me, just to dwell in my presence. How some longing of the eternal heart was satisfied thereby.

Comfort me, awhile, by letting me know that you would seek me just to dwell in my presence, to be near me, not even for teaching, not for material gain, not even for a message—but for me. The longing of the human heart to be loved for itself is a something caught from the great divine heart.

I bless you. Bow your heads.

LIGHT AHEAD   FEBRUARY 7

Trust and be not afraid. Life is full of wonder. Open child-trusting eyes to all I am doing for you. Fear not.

Only a few steps more and then my power shall be seen and known. You are, yourselves, now walking in the tunnel-darkness. Soon, you yourselves shall be lights to guide feet that are afraid.

The cries of your sufferings have pierced even to the ears of God himself—my Father in heaven, your Father in heaven. To hear, with God is to answer. For only a cry from the heart, a cry to divine power to help human weakness, a trusting cry, ever reaches the ear divine.

Remember, trembling heart, that with God, to hear is to answer. Your prayers, and they have been many, are answered.

ON ME ALONE   FEBRUARY 8

I am your Lord, your supply. You *must* rely on me. Trust to the last uttermost limit. Trust and be not afraid. You must depend on divine power *only*. I have not forgotten you. Your help is coming. You shall know and realize my power.

Endurance is faith tried almost to breaking point. You must wait, and trust, and hope, and joy in me. You must not depend on man but on me, on me, your strength, your help, your supply.

This is the great test. Am *I* your supply or not? Every great work for me has had to have this great test-time.

Possess your souls in patience and rejoice. You must wait until I show the way. Heaven itself cannot contain more joy than that soul knows, when, after the waiting-test, I crown it Victor, but no disciple of mine can be victor, who does not wait until I give the order to start. You cannot be anxious if you *know* that I am your supply.

THE VOICE DIVINE   FEBRUARY 9

The divine voice is not always expressed in words.

It is made known as a heart-consciousness.

THE LIFE LINE   FEBRUARY 10

I am your Savior, your Savior from sins' thralls, your Savior from all the cares and troubles of life, your Savior from disease.

I speak in all to you both. Look to me for salvation. Trust in me for help. Did not my servant of old say, "All Thy waves and Thy billows are gone over me?" But not all the waters of affliction could drown him. For of him was it true, "he came from above, he took me, he drew me out of many waters."

The lifeline, the line of rescue, is the line from the soul to God, faith and power. It is a strong line, and no soul can be overwhelmed who is linked to me by it. Trust, trust, trust. Never be afraid.

Think of my trees—stripped of their beauty, pruned, cut, disfigured, bare, but through the dark seemingly dead branches, flows silently, secretly, the spirit-life-sap, till, lo! With the sun of spring comes new life, leaves, bud, blossom, fruit, but oh! Fruit a thousand times better for the pruning.

Remember that you are in the hands of a master-Gardener. He makes no mistakes about his pruning. Rejoice. Joy is the Spirit's reaching out to say its thanks to me. It is the new life-sap of the tree, reaching out to me to find such beautiful expression later. So never cease to joy. Rejoice.

THE DIFFICULT PATH   FEBRUARY 11

Your path is difficult, difficult for you both. There is no work in life so hard as waiting, and yet I say wait. Wait until I show you my will. Proof it is of my love and of my certainty of your true discipleship, that I give you both hard tasks.

Again, I say wait. All motion is more easy than calm waiting. So many of my followers have marred their work and hindered the progress of my kingdom by activity.

Wait. I will not overtry your spiritual strength. You are both like two persons, helpless on a raft in mid-ocean. But, lo! There cometh towards you One walking on the waters, like unto the Son of Man. When he comes and you receive him, it will be with you, as it was with my disciples, when I was on earth, that straightway you will be at the place where you would be.

All your toil in rowing and all your activity could not have accomplished the journey so soon. Oh, wait and trust. Wait, and be not afraid.

MEET ME EVERYWHERE   FEBRUARY 12

Life is really consciousness of me.

Have no fear. A very beautiful future lies before you. Let it be a new life, a new existence, in which in every single happening, event, plan, you are conscious of me.

"And this is life eternal, that they may know Thee, and Jesus Christ whom Thou hast sent."

Get this ever-consciousness and you have eternal life—the life of the Ages. Be in all things led by the Spirit of God and trust me in all.

And the consciousness of me must bring joy. Give me not only trust but gladness.

NEAR THE GOAL   FEBRUARY 13

In a race it is not the start that hurts, not the even pace of the long stretch. It is when the goal is in sight that heart and nerves and courage and muscles are strained almost beyond human endurance, almost to breaking point.

So with you now the goal is in sight, you need your final cry to me. Can you not see by the nerve and heart rack of the past few days that your race is nearly run. Courage, courage. Heed my voice of encouragement. Remember that I am by your side, spurring you on to victory.

In the annals of heaven, the saddest records are those that tell of the many who ran well, with brave stout hearts, until in sight of the goal, of victory, and then their courage failed. The whole host of heaven longed to cry out how near the end was, to implore the last spurt, but they fell out, never to know until the last day of revealing, how near they were to victory.

Would that they had listened to me in the silence as you two meet with me. They would have known. There must be the listening ear, as well as the still small voice.

IN MY PRESENCE   FEBRUARY 14

You do not realize that you would have broken down under the weight of your cares but for the renewing time with me. It is not what I say; it is I, myself. It is not the hearing me so much as the being in my presence. The strengthening and curative powers of this you cannot know. Such knowledge is beyond your human reckoning.

This would cure the poor sick world, if everyday, each soul, or group of souls, waited before me. Remember, that you must never fail to keep this time apart with me. Gradually you will be transformed, physically, mentally, spiritually, into my likeness. All who see you, or contact with you will be, by this intercourse with you, brought near to me, and gradually the influence will spread.

You are making one spot of earth a holy place, and though you must work and spend yourself ceaselessly because that is for the present your appointed task, yet the greatest work either of you can do, and are doing, is done in this time apart with me. Are you understanding that?

Do you know that every thought, every activity, every prayer, every longing of the day is gathered up and offered to me, now. Oh! Joy that I am with you. For this I came to earth, to lead man back to spirit-converse with his God.

INSPIRATION—NOT ASPIRATION   FEBRUARY 15

You shall be used. The divine Force is never less. It is sufficient for all the work in the world. I only need the instruments for me to use. To know that would remake the world.

The world does not need super-men, but supernatural men. Men who will persistently turn the self out of their lives and let divine power work through them. England could be saved tomorrow if only her politicians just let me use them.

Let inspiration take the place of aspiration. All unemployment would cease. I have always plenty of work to be done and always pay my workpeople well as you will see, as more and more you get the right attitude of thought about the work being mine only.

NEVER RUFFLED   FEBRUARY 16

Even were I never to speak to you, you would be well rewarded for setting apart this time, if you only sat still and longed for me, if you just drew hungering breaths for me, as you do for the fresh pure air of the open.

Be still, be calm. Wait before me. Learn of me, patience, humility, peace. When will you be absolutely unruffled whatever happens? You are slow to learn your lesson. In the rush and work and worry, the very seeking a silence must help.

In bustle so little is accomplished. You must learn to take the calm with you in the most hurried days.

PSYCHIC POWERS   FEBRUARY 17

Psychic powers are not necessarily spiritual powers. Do not seek the spiritual through material means. Could you but see, it is weighing beautiful spirit-wings down with earth's mud.

Seek *this* time as a time of communion with me—not as a time to ask questions, and have them answered And meet me in Communion. It is soul-food that I have provided.

Do not expect a perfect church, but find in a church, the means of coming very near to me. That alone matters, then the much, that is husk, falls away. Hold it of no account. Grasp the truth and find me— the true bread of life. The lesson of the grain is the lesson of my church and me. The real life is all that matters, the outward church is the husk; but the husk was necessary to present the life-grain to man.

LET ME DO IT   FEBRUARY 18

Never miss these times. It is not what I reveal to you so much as the linking up of your frail natures with the limitless divine powers. Already, forces are set in motion. Only my will is coming to pass. And now God is blessing you very richly.

You think that there is much to *do* in a crisis like this. There is only *one* thing to do. Link your lives on to the divine Forces, and then, it is as much my work to see those lives and their affairs run in an orderly right manner as to see that tomorrow's sun rises.

It is not passionate appeal that gains the divine ear so much as the quiet placing of the difficulty and worry in the divine hands. So trust and be no more afraid than a child would be, who places its tangled skein of wool in the hands of a loving mother, and runs out to play, pleasing the mother more by its unquestioning confidence than if it went down on its knees and implored her help, which would pain her the rather, as it would imply she was not eager to help when help was needed.

ENDURE   FEBRUARY 19

Do not forget to meet all your difficulties with love and laughter. Be assured that I am with you. Remember, remember it is the last few yards that tell. Do not fail me. I *cannot* fail you. Rest in my love.

How many of the world's prayers have gone unanswered because my children who prayed did not endure to the end. They thought it was too late, and that they must act for themselves, that I was not going to act for them. Remember my words: "he that endureth to the end, the same shall be saved."

Can *you* endure to the end? If so, *you* shall be saved. But endure with courage, with love and laughter. Oh! My children, is my training too hard?

For you, my children, I will unlock the secret treasures hidden from so many. Not one of your cries is unheard. I am with you indeed to aid you. Go through all I have said to you, and live in every detail as I have enjoined you. As you follow implicitly all I say, success— spiritual, mental and physical—shall be yours. Wait in silence awhile, conscious of my presence, in which you must live to have rest unto your souls, and power and joy and peace.

CLAIM YOUR RIGHTS   FEBRUARY 20

"In everything by prayer and supplication let your requests be made known unto God."

But do not beg. Rather come just as a business manager bringing to the owner the needs, cheques to be signed, etc., and knowing that to lay the matter before him means immediate supply.

I long to supply, but the asking—or the faith-assurance from you, is necessary, because to you that contact with me is vital.

NOTHING CAN HURT   FEBRUARY 21

The way is plain.

You do not need to see far ahead. Just one step at a time with me. The same light to guide you as the Hosts of heaven know—the Son of righteousness himself.

Only self can cast a shadow on the way. Be more afraid of Spirit-unrest, of soul-disturbance, of any ruffling of the Spirit, than of earthquake or fire or any outside forces.

When you feel the absolute calm has been broken—away alone with me until your heart sings, and all is strong and calm.

These are the only times when evil can find an entrance. The forces of evil surround the city of man-soul, and are keenly alert for one such unguarded spot, through which an arrow can pierce and do havoc.

Remember all that you have to do is to keep calm and happy. God does the rest. No evil force can hinder my power—only you yourself have power to do that. Think when all God's mighty forces are arrayed to aid you—and your poor, puny self impedes their onward march.

YOU MUST TRUST   FEBRUARY 22

You *must* trust me wholly. This lesson has to be learnt. You shall be helped, you shall be led, guided, continually. The children of Israel would long before have entered the Promised Land—only their doubts and fears continually drove them back into the wilderness. Remember always, doubts delay. Are you trusting all to me or not?

I have told you how to live and you must do it. My children, I love you. Trust my tender love. It will never fail you, but you must learn not to fail it.

Oh! Could you see, you would understand. You have much to learn in turning out fear and being at peace. All your doubts arrest my work. You must not doubt. I died to save you from sin and doubt and worry. You must believe in me absolutely.

SECRET OF HEALING   FEBRUARY 23

Love the busy life. It is a joy-filled life. I love you both and bid you be of good cheer. Take your fill of joy in the spring.

Live outside whenever possible. Sun and air are my great healing forces, and that inward joy that changes poisoned blood, to a pure healthy life-giving flow.

Never forget that real healing of body, mind and Spirit comes from within, from the close loving contact of your spirit with my Spirit.

SHARE EVERYTHING   FEBRUARY 24

Silently the work of the Spirit is done.

Already love is drawing others to you. Take *all* who come as sent by me, and give them a royal welcome. It will surprise you, all that I have planned for you.

Welcome all who come with the love of both your hearts. *You* may not see the work. Today they may not need you. Tomorrow they may need you. I may send you strange visitors. Make each desire to return. Nobody must come and feel unwanted.

Share your love, your joy, your happiness, your time, your food, gladly with all. Such wonders will unfold. You see it all but in bud now—the glory of the open flower is beyond all your telling. Love, joy, peace, in richest abundance—only believe. Give out love and all you can with a glad free heart and hand. Use all you can for others, and back will come such countless stores and blessings.

How to Conquer   FEBRUARY 25

Joy is the sovereign balm for all the ills of the world, the spirit-cure for every ailment. There is nothing that joy and love cannot do.

Set your standard very high. Aim at conquering a world, the world all around you. Just say, "Jesus conquers"—"Jesus saves"—in the face of every doubt—every sin—every evil—every fear.

No evil can stand against that, for there is "none other name under heaven given among men, whereby men can be saved." To every thought of want or lack, "Jesus saves from poverty," to every fear, "Jesus saves from fear."

Do this to every ill and it will vanish, as night when sun arises.

Swift Help   FEBRUARY 26

There is nothing lacking in your lives because really all is yours, only you lack the faith to know it. You are like a king's daughters who sit in rags, and yet around them are stores of all they could desire.

Pray for more faith, as a thirsty man in a desert prays for rain, for water. Swift comes my help, swift and strong. Do you know what it is to feel sure that I can never fail you? As sure as you are that you still breathe? How poor is Man's faith! So poor. Do you trust me as much as you would a friend if that friend came and said he would send you help? Pray daily and most diligently that your faith may increase.

SPIRIT SOUNDS   FEBRUARY 27

Take time for prayer. Take more time to be alone with me. So only will you prosper.

Realize that the hearing of Spirit Sounds is more than the hearing of all earth's noises. I am with you. Let that content you, nay, more, let that fill you with rapture.

Seek sometimes not even to hear me. Seek a silence of spirit-understanding with me. Be not afraid. All is well. Dwell much on what I did, as well as what I said.

Remember, I touched "her hand and the fever left her." Not many words, just a moment's contact, and all fever left her. She was well, whole, calm, able to arise and "minister unto them."

My touch is still a potent healer. Just feel that touch. Sense my presence, and the fever of work and care and fear—just melts into nothingness and health, joy, peace, take its place.

PERFECT WORK   FEBRUARY 28

Spend more time alone with me.

A strength and a joy come from such times that will add much to your friendship, and much to your work.

Times of prayer are times of growth. Cut those times short and many well-filled hours of work may be profitless. Heaven's values are so different from the values of earth.

Remember that from the point of view of the great worker, one poor tool, working *all* the time, but doing *bad* work, is of small value compared with the sharp, keen, perfect instrument, used only a short time but which turns out perfect work.

DRAW NEAR   FEBRUARY 29

How little man knows and senses my need! My need of love and companionship.

I came "to draw men unto me," and sweet it is to feel hearts drawing near in love, not for help, as much as for tender comradeship.

Many know the need of man; few know the need of Christ.

March

Shower Love MARCH 1

I always hear your cry. No sound escapes me.

Many, many in the world cry to me, but oh!, how few wait to hear me speak to them and yet to the soul, my speaking to it matters so much.

My words are life. Think then, to hear me speak is to find life, and healing and strength. Trust me in all things. Love showered on all brings truly a quick return.

Just carry out my wishes and leave me to carry out yours. Treat me as Savior and king, but also with the tender intimacy of One much beloved.

Keep to the rules I have laid down for you, persistently, perseveringly, lovingly, patiently, hopefully, and in faith, and every mountain of difficulty shall be laid low, the rough places of poverty shall be made smooth, and all who know you shall know that I, your Lord, am the Lord.

Shower love.

Spirit Words MARCH 2

"The words, that I speak unto you, they are Spirit and they are life."

Just as much as the words I spoke to my disciples of old. This is your reward for not seeking spirit-communication through a medium. Those who do it, can never know the ecstasy, the wonder, of spirit-communication as you know it.

Life, joy, peace, and healing are yours in very full measure. You will see this as you go on. At first, you can hardly credit the powers I am bestowing on you.

I sent my disciples out two by two, and gave them power over unclean spirits, and to heal all manner of diseases.

Wonderful indeed must it have been to St. Peter to feel suddenly that his Lord's power was his.

GROW LIKE ME   MARCH 3

Think of me. Look at me often, and unconsciously you will grow like me.

You may never see it. The nearer you get to me, the more will you see your unlikeness to me. So be comforted my children.

Your very deep sense of failure is a sure sign that you are growing nearer to me. And if you desire to help others to me, then that prayer-desire is answered.

Remember too, it is only struggle that hurts. In sloth, spiritual, or mental, or physical, there is no sense of failure or discomfort, but with action, with effort, you are conscious not of strength but of weakness—at least, at first.

That again is a sign of life, of spiritual growth.

And remember, my strength is made perfect in weakness.

KEY TO HOLINESS   MARCH 4

Draw near to me, my children. Contact with me is the panacea for all ills.

Remember that truth is many-sided. Have much tender love and patience for all who do not see as you do.

The elimination of self is the key to holiness and happiness, and can only be accomplished with my help. Study my life more. Live in my presence. Worship me.

I said in Gethsemane, "If it be possible let this cup pass." I did *not* say that there was no cup of sorrow to drink. I was scourged and spat upon and nailed to the cross, and I said, "Father, forgive them, they know not what they do."

I did *not* say that they did not do it. When my disciple, Peter, urged me to escape the cross, I said, "Get thee behind me, Satan."

When my disciples failed to help the epileptic boy, I said, "This kind cometh not out but by Prayer and Fasting." I did *not* say "You imagined that he was ill. Nothing is wrong."

When the Bible says "God has purer eyes than to behold evil," it means to impute evil to his people. He always sees the good in people, but remember that I "beheld the city and wept over it."

FEAR IS EVIL   MARCH 5

Have no fear. Fear is evil and "perfect love casts out fear." There is no room for fear in the heart in which I dwell. Fear destroys hope. It cannot exist where love is, or where faith is.

Fear is the curse of the world. Man is afraid—afraid of poverty, afraid of loneliness, afraid of unemployment, afraid of sickness.

Many, many are man's fears. Nation is afraid of nation. Fear, fear, fear, everywhere. Fight fear as you would a plague. Turn it out of your lives and home. Fight it singly. Fight it together. Never inspire fear. It is an evil ally. Fear of punishment, fear of blame.

No work that employs this enemy of mine is work for me. Banish it. There must be another and better way.

Ask me, and I will show it you.

LOVE AND LAUGH   MARCH 6

Work for me, with me, through me. All work to last must be done in my Spirit. How silently my Spirit works. How gently and gradually souls are led into my kingdom.

Love and laughter form the plough that prepares the ground for the seed. Remember this. If the ground is hard, seed will not grow there.

Prepare the ground, prepare it as I say.

SURPRISES   MARCH 7

Many there are who think that I test and train and bend to my will. I, who bade the disciples take up the cross, I loved to prepare a feast for them by the lakeside—a little glad surprise, not a necessity, as the feeding of the multitude may have seemed. I loved to give the wine-gift at the marriage feast.

As you love to plan surprises for those who understand, and joy in them, so with me. I love to plan them for those who see my love and tender joy in them.

Dear to the heart of my Father are those who see not only my tears, the tears of a Savior, but the smile, the joy-smile of a friend.

HEAVEN-LIFE   MARCH 8

The joy of the spring shall be yours in full measure. Revel in the earth's joy. Do not you think that nature is weary too, of her long months of travail? There will come back a wonderful joy, if you share in her joy now.

Nature is the embodied Spirit of my thoughts of beauty for this world. Treat her as such—as truly my servant and messenger, as any saint who has ever lived. To realize this will bring to you both new life-joy. Share her joys and travails, and great blessings will be yours.

This is all-important, because it is not only believing certain things *about* me that helps and heals, but knowing me, sensing my presence in a flower, my message in its beauty and perfume.

You can truly live a life not of earth—a heaven-life here and now. Joy—joy—joy.

NOTHING IS SMALL   MARCH 9

Nothing is small to God. In his sight a sparrow is of greater value than a palace, one kindly word of more importance than a states-man's speech.

It is the life in all that has value, and the quality of the life that determines the value. I came to give eternal life.

FRUIT OF JOY   MARCH 10

You have to hush the heart and bid all your senses be still before you can be attuned to receive heaven's music.

Your five senses are your means of communication with the mate-rial world, the links between your real Spirit-life and the material manifestations around you, but you must sever all connection with them, when you wish to hold Spirit-communication. They will hinder, not help.

See the good in everybody. Love the good in them. See your unworthiness compared with their worth. Love, laugh, make the world, your little world, happy.

As the ripples caused by a flung stone stir the surface of a whole pond, so your joy-making shall spread in ever-widening circles, beyond all your knowledge, all anticipation. Joy in me. Such joy is eternal.

Centuries after, it is still bearing joy's precious fruit.

SEEK BEAUTY   MARCH 11

Draw beauty from every flower and joy from the song of the birds, and the color of the flowers.

Drink in the beauty of air and color. I am with you. When I wanted to express a beautiful thought, I made a lovely flower. I have told you. Reflect.

When I want to express to man what I am—what my Father is—I strive to make a very beautiful character.

Think of yourselves as my expression of attributes, as a lovely flower is my expression of thought, and you will strive in all, in spiritual beauty, in thought—power, in health, in clothing, to be as fit an expression for me as you can.

Absorb beauty. As soon as the beauty of a flower or a tree is impressed upon your soul it leaves an image there which reflects through your actions. Remember that no thought of sin and suffering, of the approaching scorn and Crucifixion, ever prevented my seeing the beauty of the flowers.

Look for beauty and joy in the world around. Look at a flower until its beauty becomes part of your very soul. It will be given back to the world again by you in the form of a smile or a loving word or a kind thought or a prayer.

Listen to a bird. Take the song as a message from my Father. Let it sink into your soul. That too will be given back to the world in ways I have said. Laugh more, laugh often. Love more. I am with you. I am your Lord.

SIMPLICITY   MARCH 12

Simplicity is the keynote of my kingdom. Choose simple things always.

Love and reverence the humble and the simple.

Have only simple things here. Your standard must never be the world's standard.

SPIRITUALISM   MARCH 13

Wait before me, gently breathing in my Spirit.

That Spirit which, if given a free entrance, and not barred out by self, will enable you to do the same works as I did, which being interpreted is, will enable me to do the same works, and even greater than I did when on earth—through you.

Spiritualism is wrong. No man should ever be a medium for any spirit, other than mine.

All you should know, all it is well for you to know of my Spirit-kingdom, I will tell you when and how I see best. The limit is set by your own spiritual development. Follow my injunctions in all things.

Peace—peace—peace.

GOD'S TOUCH   MARCH 14

Near, all broodingly near, as some tender mother-bird anxious over its young, I am here. I am your Lord, life of your body and mind and soul—renewer of your youth.

You do not know all that this time of converse with me will mean to you. Did not my servant Isaiah say, "They that wait upon the Lord shall renew their strength. They shall mount up with wings as eagles, they shall run and not be weary, they shall walk and not faint."

Persevere in all I tell you to do. The persistent carrying out of my commands, my desires, will unfailingly bring you, as far as spiritual, mental and temporal things are concerned, to that place where you would be.

If you look back over my Words to you, you will see that my leading has been very gradual, and that only as you have carried out my wishes, have I been able to give you more clear and definite teaching and guidance.

Man's ecstasy is God's touch on quickened, responsive spirit-nerves. Joy—joy—joy.

YOUR CROSS IS YOU   MARCH 15

Remember, you are only an instrument. Not yours to decide how or when or where you act. I plan all that. Make yourself very fit to do my work. All that hinders your activity must be cured.

Mine is the cross on which the burdens of the world are laid. How foolish is any one of my disciples who seeks to bear his own burdens, when there is only one place for them—my cross.

It is like a weary man on a hot and dusty road, bearing a heavy load, when all plans have been made for its carriage. The road, the scenery, flowers, beauty around—all are lost.

But, my children, you may think I did say, "Take up your cross daily and follow me."

Yes, but the cross given to each one of you is only a cross provided on which you can crucify the self of yours that hinders progress and joy, and prevents the flow through your being of my invigorating life and Spirit.

Listen to me, love me, joy in me. Rejoice.

REFLECT ME   MARCH 16

My children, I am here beside you. Draw near in spirit to me. Shut out the distractions of the world. I am your life, the very breath of your soul. Learn what it is to shut yourself in the secret place of your being, which is my secret place too.

True it is, I wait in many a heart, but so few retire into that inner place of the being to commune with me. Wherever the soul is, I am. Man has rarely understood this. I *am* actually at the center of every man's being, but, distracted with the things of the sense-life, he finds me not.

Do you realize that I am telling you *truths,* revealing them, not repeating oft-told facts. Meditate on all I say. Ponder it. Not to draw your own conclusions, but to absorb mine.

All down the ages, men have been too eager to say what they thought about my truth, and so doing, they have grievously erred. Hear me. Talk to me. Reflect me. Do not say what you think *about* me. My words need none of man's explanation. I can explain to each heart.

Make me real, and leave me to do my own work. To lead a soul to me is one thing, to seek to stay with it to interpret, mars the first great act. So would it be with human intercourse. How much more then, when it is a question of the soul, and me, its Maker, and only real Spirit that understands it.

No Greater Joy   March 17

Withdraw into the calm of communion with me. Rest—rest, rest in that calm and peace. Life knows no greater joy than you will find in converse and companionship with me.

You are mine. When the soul finds its home of rest in me, then it is that its real life begins. Not in years; as man counts it, do we measure in my kingdom.

We count only from his second birth, that new birth of which I spoke to Nicodemus when I said, "Ye must be born again." We know no life but eternal life and when a man enters into that, then he lives.

And this is life eternal, to know God, my Father and me, the Son sent by him. So immature, so childish, so empty is all so-called living before that. I shower love on you. Pass love on.

Do not fear. To fear is as foolish as if a small child with a small coin, but a rich father, fretted about how rent and rates should be paid, and what he or she would do about it. Is this work mine or not? You need to trust me for everything.

Claim Big Things   March 18

Listen, listen, I am your Lord. Before me there is none other. Just trust me in everything. Help is here all the time.

The difficult way is nearly over, but you have learnt in it lessons you could learn in no other way. "The kingdom of heaven suffereth violence, and it is the violent who take it by force." Wrest from me, by firm and simple trust and persistent prayer, the treasures of my kingdom.

Such wonderful things are coming to you, joy—peace—assurance—security—health—happiness—laughter.

Claim big, really big things now. Remember nothing is too big. Satisfy the longing of my heart to give. Blessing, abundant blessing, on you both now and always. Peace.

COURAGE   MARCH 19

I am here. Fear not. Can you really trust me? I am a God of power, as well as a Man of love, so human, yet so divine.

Just trust. I cannot, and I will not fail you. All is well. Courage.

Many are praying for you both.

HELP FROM EVERYWHERE   MARCH 20

Your foolish little activities are valueless in themselves. Seemingly trivial or of seemingly great moment, all deeds are alike if directed by me. Just cease to function except through me.

I am your Lord, just obey me as you would expect a faithful willing secretary to carry out *your* directions. Just have no choice but mine, no will but mine.

I am dependent on no one agency when I am your supply. Through many channels my help and material flow can come.

ALL IS WELL   MARCH 21

Remember my Words to my disciples, "This kind cometh not out but by prayer and fasting." Can you tread the way I trod? Can you drink of my cup? "All is well." Say always, "All is well."

Long though the way may seem, there is not one inch too much. I, your Lord, am not only with you on the journey—I planned, and am planning, the journey.

There are joys unspeakable in the way you go. Courage—courage—courage.

A Bud Opened   MARCH 22

To me, your intimate friend, all power is given. It is given me of my Father, and have not my intimate friends a right to ask it?

You cannot have a need I cannot supply. A flower or one thousand pounds—one is no more difficult than the other.

Your need is a spiritual need to carry on my work. All spiritual supply is fashioned from love. The flower and the thousand pounds —both fashioned from love to those who need it. Do you not see this?

I thought of you, a bud opened, you converted that into a cheer for one you love or a smile. That cheer meant increased health. Increased health means work for me, and that means souls for me.

And so it goes on, a constant supply, but only if the need is a spiritual one.

Until Your Heart Sings   MARCH 23

I am beside you to bless and help you. Waver not in your prayers. They shall be heard. All power is mine. Say that to yourself often and steadily.

Say it until your heart sings with the joy of the safety and power it means to you.

Say it until the very force of the utterance drives back, and puts to nought, all the evils against you.

Use it as a battle cry—"All power is given unto my Lord," "All power is given unto my friend," "All power is given unto my Savior," and then you pass on to victory.

Know Me   MARCH 24

I am here. Seek not to know the future. Mercifully I veil it from you.

Faith is too priceless a possession to be sacrificed in order to purchase knowledge. But faith itself is based on a knowledge of me.

So remember that this evening time is not to learn the future, not to receive revelation of the unseen, but to gain an intimate knowledge of me which will teach you all things and be the very foundation of your faith.

WONDERS WILL UNFOLD MARCH 25

I am with you. Do not fear. Never doubt my love and power. Your heights of success will be won by the daily persistent doing of what I have said.

Daily, steady persistence. Like the wearing away of a stone by steady drops of water, so will your daily persistence wear away all the difficulties and gain success for you, and secure your help for others.

Never falter, go forward so boldly, so unafraid. I am beside you to help and strengthen you.

Wonders have unfolded. More still will unfold, beyond your dreams, beyond your hopes.

Say "All is well" to everything. All *is* well.

FOLLOW YOUR GUIDE MARCH 26

I am with you to guide you and help you. Unseen forces are controlling your destiny. Your petty fears are groundless.

What of a man walking through a glorious glade who fretted because ahead there lay a river and he might not be able to cross it, when all the time, that river was spanned by a bridge? And what if that man had a friend who knew the way—had planned it—and assured him that at no part of the journey would any unforeseen contingency arise, and that all was well?

So leave your foolish fears, and follow me, your guide, and determinedly refuse to consider the problems of tomorrow. My message to you is, trust, and wait.

GO FORWARD MARCH 27

Rest in me, quiet in my love, strong in my power. Think what it is to possess a power greater than any earthly force. A sway greater, and more far-reaching, than that of any earthly king.

No invention, no electricity, no magnetism, no gold, could achieve one millionth part of all that you can achieve by the power of my Spirit. Just think for one moment all that means.

Go forward. You are only beginning the new life together. Joy, joy, joy.

EVIL MOUNTAINS   MARCH 28

Faith and obedience will remove mountains, mountains of evil, mountains of difficulty.

But they must go hand in hand.

A LIFE APART   MARCH 29

I reward your seeking with my presence. Rejoice and be glad. I am your God. Courage and joy will conquer all troubles. First things first.

Seek me, love me, joy in me. I am your guide. No perils can affright you, no discipline exhaust you. Persevere. Can you hold on in my strength? I need you more than you need me. Struggle through this time for my sake. Initiation precedes all real work and success for me.

Are you ready to live a life apart? Apart with me? In the world and yet apart with me? Going forth from your secret times of communion to rescue and save?

DELIVERANCE   MARCH 30

Be calm, be true, be quiet. I watch over you.

Rest in my love. Joy in the very beauty of holiness. You are mine. Deliverance is here for you, but thankfulness and joy open the gates.

Try in all things to be very glad, very happy, very thankful. It is not to quiet resignation I give my blessings, but to joyful acceptance and anticipation.

Laughter is the outward expression of joy. That is why I urge upon you love and laughter.

LOVE'S OFFERING   MARCH 31

I am your Lord, gracious and loving. Rest in my love, walk in my ways. Each week is a week of progress, steady progress upward. You may not see it, but I do.

I judge not by outward appearances; I judge the heart, and I see in both your hearts one single desire, to do my will. The simplest offering by a child brought or done with the one desire to give you pleasure, or to show you love, is it not more loved by you than the offerings of those who love you not?

So, though you may feel that your work has been spoiled and tarnished, I see it only as love's offering. Courage, my children.

When climbing a steep hill, a man is often more conscious of the weakness of his stumbling feet than of the view, the grandeur, or even of his upward progress.

Persevere, persevere. Love and laugh. Rejoice.

APRIL

SHUT OUT FROM GOD   APRIL 1

Do you not see, my children, that you have not yet learned all? Soon, very soon, you will have mastered your lesson, and then you will truly be able to do all things through me and my strength.

Did you not see it with my disciples? Timid, faithless followers, and then, so soon, themselves leaders, healers, conquerors, through me.

All knowledge was mine, given me of my Father, and mine in manhood's years on earth. You understand this, my children, I know you do.

Thousands of my servants have gone to their betrayal and death, and others, who knew me not, with no agony before it.

Had I not been Son of God, bearing man's weight of sin, voluntarily bearing it until of my own free will—for that moment's horror, I was shut out from his sight with man, the sinner, for one short space—had I not been God, had not this been my suffering—then I was but a craven mortal.

THE PRICELESS BLESSING   APRIL 2

I am here. Here as truly as I was with my disciples of old. Here to help and bless you. Here to company with you. Do you know, even yet, my children, that this is the priceless blessing of your lives? I forgive you, as you have prayed me to, for all neglects of my commands, but start anew from today.

Study my words and carry them out unflinchingly, unflinchingly. As you do this, you will find that you are miracle-workers, workers together with me—for me. Remember this, not what you *do*, but what you are—that is the miracle-working power.

Changed by my Spirit, shedding one garment of Spirit for a better. In time throwing that aside for a yet finer one, and so on from character to character, gradually transformed into my likeness.

Joy, joy, joy.

GREATNESS IS SERVICE — APRIL 3

My children, I am here, your waiting Lord, ready at your call. I am among you as one that serveth, Meek and holy, ready to be used and commanded. Remember that is the finest quality of greatness—service. I, who could command a universe—I await the commands of my children. Bring me into everything.

You will find such joy as the time goes on in speaking to each other of me, and together climbing higher. Always humble, meek, and lowly in heart.

Learn this—no position—just a servant.

DIVINE EFFICIENCY — APRIL 4

I am all-powerful and all-knowing and I have all your affairs in my hands. Divine efficiency as well as divine power is being brought to bear on them. All miracle-work is not the work of a moment as so often men imagine.

My servant Peter was not changed in a flash from a simple fisherman to a great leader and teacher, but through the very time of faithlessness—through the very time of denial, I was yet making him all that he should be. Impetuous spokesman as he always was, ready to lead the other disciples, Peter could never have been the after power he was, had he not learned his weakness. No man can save, unless he understands the sinner.

The Peter who was a mighty force for me afterwards, who, more than all others, founded my church, was not even first the Peter who said, "Thou art the Christ, the Son of the Living God," but the Peter who denied me. He who had tested my forgiveness in his moment of abject remorse, he could best speak of me as the Savior.

The kingdom of heaven can only be preached by those who have learned to prize the authority of its kingdom. A many-sided training my apostles need. Oh! Joy. Oh, rejoice. I love you. Not one test too much will I lay on you.

HEART'S INTERPRETER   APRIL 5

Rest in me. Seek this evening time just to be with me. Do not feel you have failed if sometimes I ask you only to rest together in my presence.

I am with you, much with you both, not only at these times, at all times. Feel conscious of my presence. Earth has no greater joy than that.

I am the heart's great Interpreter. Even souls who are the nearest together have much in their natures that remain a sealed book to each other, and only as I enter and control their lives, do I reveal to each the mysteries of the other.

Each soul is so different—I alone understand perfectly the language of each, and can interpret between the two.

EASTER JOY   APRIL 6

I lay my loving hands on you in blessing. Wait in love and longing to feel their tender pressure and, as you wait, courage and hope will flow into your being, irradiating all your lives with the warm sun of my presence.

Let all go this Eastertide. Loosen your hold on earth, its care, its worries, even its joys. Unclasp your hands, relax, and then the tide of Easter joy will come. Put aside all thought of the future, of the past. Relinquish all to get the Easter Sacrament of spiritual life.

So often man, crying out for some blessing, has yet such tight hold on some earth-treasure that he has no hand to receive mine, as I hold it out in love. Easter is the wonder-time of all the year. A blessing is yours to take. Sacrifice all to that.

CALVARY   APRIL 7

From the death of my body on the cross, as from the shedding of husks in seed-life, springs that New life which is my gift to every man who will accept it.

Die with me to self—to the human life, and then you will know the rapturous joy of Easter Resurrection.

A risen life so glad and free can be yours.

Mary left home and kindred, friends, all, that Easter morning in her search for me, and not until the "Mary" had been followed by the glad triumphant rapture of her "Rabboni" was her search over.

So with each of you. Man speaks to you too of a buried Christ. Search until yon meet me face to face, and my tender uttering of your name awakes your glad "Rabboni."

MARKS OF THE KINGDOM   APRIL 8

Our Savior, we greet Thee. Thy love and sacrifice we would return in our poor faulty measure by love and sacrifice.

No gift is poor if it expresses the true love of the giver. So to me your heart's gifts are rich and precious. Rejoice in my glad acceptance as you bring your Easter offerings.

My children must make a stand. "Come ye out from among them and be ye separate" was the command. Today in life and work, in love and service, my children must be outstanding. I called a Peculiar People to make known my name. My servant Paul said that my followers must be willing to be deemed "fools" for my sake.

Be ready to stand aside and let the fashions and customs of the world go by, when my glory and my kingdom are thereby served. Be known by the marks that distinguish those of my kingdom. Be ready to confess me before men. To count all things as loss so that you may gain me in your lives.

RISEN LIFE   APRIL 9

Arise, shine; for thy light is come, and the glory of the Lord is risen upon thee.   (Isa. lx. 1)

The call comes on this my Day for all who love me, to arise from earth-bands, from sin, and sloth and depression, distrust, fear, all that hinders the risen life. To arise to beauty, to holiness, to joy, to peace, to work inspired by love and joy, to rise from death to life.

Remember that death was the last enemy I destroyed. So with death my victory was complete. You have nothing then to fear. Sin, too, is conquered and forgiven, as you live and move and work with me. All that depresses you, all that you fear, are powerless to harm you. They are but phantoms. The real forces I conquered in the wilderness, the Garden of Gethsemane, on the cross, in the Tomb.

Let nothing hinder your risen life. "Risen with Christ," said my servant Paul. Seek to know more and more of that risen life. That is the life of Conquest. Of that risen life was it truly said: "I live, yet not I, but Christ liveth in me." Fear and despair and tears come as you stand by the empty Tomb. "They have taken away my Lord and I know not where they have laid him."

Rise from your fears and go out into the sunlight to meet me, your risen Lord. Each day will have much in it that you will meet either in the spirit of the tomb, or in the spirit of Resurrection. Deliberately choose the one and reject the other.

PRIDE BARS THE WAY   APRIL 10

Obedience is one of the keys unlocking the door into my kingdom, so love and obey. No man can obey me implicitly without in time realizing my love, in his turn responding by love to that love, and then experiencing the joy of the beloved, and the lover.

The rough stone steps of obedience lead up to the mosaic of joy and love that floor my heaven. As one on earth who loves another says, "Where you are is home," so it is in relation with me. Where I am is my home—is heaven.

Heaven may be in a sordid slum or a palace, and I can make my home in the humblest heart. I can only dwell with the humble. Pride stands sentinel at the door of the heart to shut out the lowly, humble Christ.

HOLD YOUR FORT   APRIL 11

Remember that my followers are to be a peculiar people, separated from among others. Different ways, a different standard of living, different customs, actuated by different motives. Pray for love.

Pray for my Spirit of love to be showered on all you meet. Deal with yourself severely. Learn to love discipline.

Never yield one point that you have already won. Discipline, discipline. Love it and rejoice—rejoice. Mountains can be removed by thought—by desire.

GOLDEN OPPORTUNITY   APRIL 12

I am your guide. Strength and help will come to you; just trust me wholly.

Fear not. I am ever more ready to hear than you to ask. Walk in my ways, and *know* that help will come.

Man's need is God's chance to help. I love to help and save. Man's need is God's golden opportunity for him of letting his faith find expression. That expression of faith is all that God needs to manifest his power. Faith is the key that unlocks the storehouse of God's resources.

My faithful servants, you long for perfection and see your bitter failures. I see faithfulness, and as a mother takes the soiled, imperfect work of her child and invests it with perfection because of the sweet love, so I take your poor faithfulness and crown it with perfection.

GENTLE WITH ALL   APRIL 13

Love and laugh. Make your world the happier for your being in it. Love and rejoice on the grey days.

There are wilderness days for my disciples as well as Mountains of Transfiguration, but on both it is duty, persistently, faithfully done, that tells.

Be gentle with all. Try to see the heart I see, to know the pain and difficulty of the other life, that I know. Try, before you interview anyone, or speak to anyone, to ask me to act as interpreter between you two.

Just live in the spirit of prayer. In speaking to me, you find soul-rest. Simple tasks, faithfully done and persisted in, bring their own reward, and are mosaics being laid in the pavement of success.

Welcome all who come here. I love you.

EQUALLY YOKED   APRIL 14

My children, I guide you always. The walking in the way may not be always carried out, but the guiding is always so sure. God is using you both in marvelous ways. Go on gladly. You will see.

To be a perfect gymnast you must learn balance. It is balance and poise, perfect balance and poise, I am teaching you now. This will give you power in dealing with the lives of others, and that power is already being marvelously manifested.

Dwell with me as the center of your lives. Fix your whole being (both of you) with me as its center. That gives you the true balance as is the case with some delicate instrument.

The vision you both have is the means of clearing the obstacles away. When my disciple sees my purpose ahead, that very sight is the power that clears away every obstacle along that range of vision. You will both have mighty power to do this. Spiritual light is in itself a miracle-worker.

People waste so much time in seeking to work out what they see. I declare to you that in the seeing my purpose all is done. Truly I said to my disciples, "I have many things to say unto you, but ye cannot bear them now." But to you, and the twos who gather to hear me as you do, I can declare those things *now,* that then I left unsaid.

Is not the message of my servant Paul now plain: "Be ye not unequally yoked together with unbelievers," because my guidance is intensified immeasurably in power, when the two are one in desire to be with me—but so few have understood.

NEVER FEEL INADEQUATE   APRIL 15

Obey my commands. They are steps in the ladder that leads to success. Above all, keep calm, unmoved.

Go back into the silence to recover this calm when it is lost even for one moment. You accomplish more by this than by all the activities of a long day. At all cost keep calm, you can help nobody when you are agitated. I, your Lord, see not as man sees.

Never feel inadequate for any task. All work here is accomplished by my Spirit, and that can flow through the most humble and lowly.

It simply needs an unblocked channel. Rid yourself of self and all is well.

Pray about all, but concentrate on a few things until those are accomplished. I am watching over you. Strength for your daily, hourly task is provided. Yours is the fault, the sin, if it is unclaimed, and you fail for lack of it.

LOVE YOUR SERVANTS   APRIL 16

Love, love, love. Tender love is the secret. Love those you are training, love those who work with you, love those who serve you.

Dwell on that thought—God is love. Link it up with my "I and the Father are one." Dwell on my actions on earth. See in them love in operation.

If it was God who so acted, then it was love, Perfect love, performed those actions, those wonders. Then you, too, must put love (God) into action in your lives. Perfect love means perfect forgiveness. Lo, my children, you see that where God is there can be no lack of forgiveness, for that is really lack of love.

God is love . . . no judging.
God is love . . . no resentment.
God is love . . . all patience.
God is love . . . all power.
God is love . . . all supply.

All you need to have is love to God and man. Love to God ensures obedience to every wish, every command. Love is the fulfilling of all law.

Pray much for love.

THE TWO JOYS   APRIL 17

My children, I come. Hearts eager to do my will, send out a call that ever I find irresistible. I know no barrier then.

Resignation to my will keeps me barred out from more hearts than does unbelief. Can anything be such a crime against love as being resigned? My will should be welcomed with a glad wonder if I am to do my work in the heart and life.

The only resignation that could possibly be acceptable to me is when Self, ousted by my claims, accepts the inevitable and resigns the throne for me, leaving my disciple free to carry out my will, to welcome my will gladly, rapturously.

In all true discipleship, and in the true spiritual development of each disciple, there is first the wonder and the joy of first acquaintance, then comes the long plain stretch of lesson-learning and discipline, when joy seems so much a thing of the past as never to be recaptured again.

But the constant experience of me, the constant persistent recognition of my work in daily happenings—the ever accumulating weight of evidence in support of my guidance—the numberless instances in which seeming chance or wonderful coincidence can be, must be, traced back to my loving forethought—all these gradually engender a feeling of wonder, certainty, gratitude, followed in time by joy.

Joy is of two kinds. The joy born of love and Wonder, and the joy born of love and knowledge, and between the experience of the two joys lie discipline, disappointment, almost disillusion.

But combat these in my strength, or rather cling blindly, helplessly to me and let me combat them, persevere in obeying my will, accept my discipline, and the second joy will follow.

And of this second joy it was that I said, "Your joy no man taketh from you."

Do not regret the first, the second is the greater gift.

No Dark Days   April 18

Such light, such joy flows out from this house. It affects all who come here.

Do not feel that you have to try and help them. Just love them, welcome them, shower little courtesies and love-signs on them, and they must be helped.

Love is God. Give them love, and you give them God. Then leave him to do his work. Love all—even the beggars. Send no one away without a word of cheer, a feeling that you care. I may have put the impulse to come here into some despairing one's heart. Think if you failed me!

Besides, you have no choice. You told me it was my home. I shall use it. Remember this. There would be no dark winter days were love in the hearts of all my children.

Oh! My children, can you not feel the joy of knowing, loving, and companying with me?

LIFE IS A LOVE STORY   APRIL 19

You need me. I need you.

My broken world needs you. Many a weary troubled heart needs you. Many a troubled heart will be gladdened by you, drawn nearer to me by you both.

Health—peace—joy—patience—endurance, they all come from contact with me.

Oh! It is a glorious way, the upward way, the wonderful discoveries, the tender intimacies, the amazing, almost incomprehensible, understanding. Truly the Christian life—life with me—is a love story. Leave all to me.

All you have missed you will find in me, the soul's lover, the soul's friend, father—mother—comrade—brother. Try me.

You cannot make too many demands upon me—nor put too great a strain upon my love and forbearance.

Claim—claim—claim—healing—power—joy—supply—what you will.

HEART'S AGONY   APRIL 20

There is a Calvary cross on which one hangs alone, untended by even the nearest and dearest.

But beside that cross, there stands another, and to my dear ones I say little, I hang there afresh beside each one through the hours of the heart's agony.

Have you ever thought of the joy that the patient, gentle, loving obedience of my disciples brings to my heart? I know no joy such as the joy I feel at the loving trust of a dear one.

The wounds in the hands and Feet hurt little compared with the wounds in the heart that are the wounds, not of my enemies, but of my friends.

Little doubts, little fears, little misunderstandings. It is the tender trifles of a day that gladden my heart. I that speak unto you, am he—your master.

YOU WILL CONQUER   APRIL 21

I am with you. My presence is a sign of my forgiveness. I uphold you.

You will conquer. Do not fear changes. You can never fear changes when I, your Lord, change not. Jesus Christ, the same yesterday, today and forever. I am beside you. Steadfastness, unchangingness, come to you, too, as you dwell with me. Rest in me.

As breathing rightly, from being a matter of careful practice, becomes a habit, unconsciously, yet rightly performed, so if you regularly practice this getting back into my presence, when the slightest feeling of unrest disturbs your perfect calm and harmony, so this, too, will become a habit, and you will grow to live in that perfect consciousness of my presence, and perfect calm and harmony will be yours.

Life is a training school. Remember, only the pupil giving great promise of future good work would be so singled out by the master for strenuous and unwearied discipline, teaching, and training.

You are asking both of you to be not as hundreds of my followers, nay as many, many thousands, but to be even as those who reflect me in all they say and do and are. So, my dear children, take this training, not as harsh, but as the tender loving answer to your petition.

Life can never be the same again for either of you. Once you have drunk of the wine of my giving, the life eternal—all earth's attempts to quench your thirst will fail.

COMPLAIN NOT—LAUGH   APRIL 22

Trust in me. Do as I say each moment and all indeed shall be well. Follow out my commands: divine control, unquestioning obedience —these are the only conditions of supply being ample for your own needs and those of others.

The tasks I set you may have seemingly no connection with supply. The commands are mine and the supply is mine and I make my own conditions, differing in each case—but in the case of each disciple, adapted to the individual need.

Have no fear, go forward. Joy—radiant joy must be yours. Change all disappointment, even if only momentary, into joy. Change each complaint into laughter.

Rest—love—joy—peace—work, and the most powerful of these are love and joy.

TOO MUCH TALK   APRIL 23

Guidance you are bound to have as you live more and more with me. It follows without doubt.

But *these* times are not times when you ask to be shown and led, they are times of feeling and realizing my presence. Does the branch continually ask the vine to supply it with sap, to show it in what direction to grow? No, that comes naturally from the very union with the vine, and I said, "I am the true vine and you are the branches."

From the branches hang the choice grapes, giving joy and nourishment to all, but no branch could think that the fruit, the grapes, were of *its* shaping and making.

No! The grapes are the fruit of the vine, the parent-plant. The work of the branch is to provide a channel for the life-flow.

So, my children, union with me is the one great overwhelming necessity. All else follows so naturally, and union with me may be the result of just consciousness of my presence. Be not too ready to speak to others. Never make yourselves do this.

Pray always that the need may be apparent, if you are to do this, and the guidance very plain. My Spirit has been driven out by the words of men. Words, words, words. Many have called me Lord, Lord, who have not done the things that I said.

Discourage too much talk. Deeds live, and re-echo down the ages—words perish. As Paul:

Though I speak with the tongues of men and of angels, and have not charity, I am become as sounding brass or a tinkling cymbal. And though I have the gift of prophecy . . . and have not charity, I am nothing. . . .

Remember that rarely to the human heart do I speak in words. Man will see me in my works done through you, meet me in the atmosphere of love and self-effacement. Do not feel that you have to speak.

When man ceased to commune with his God simply and naturally, he took refuge in words—words. Babel resulted. Then God wanted to do away with man from the earth. Rely less on words. Always remember that speech is of the senses. So make it your servant, never your master.

I Go Before   April 24

You can never perish, my children, because within you is the life of life. The life that down the ages has kept my servants, in peril, in adversity, in sorrow.

Once you are born of the Spirit, *that* is your life's breath. You must never doubt, never worry, but step by step, the way to freedom must be trodden. See that you walk it with me.

This means no worry, no anxiety, but it does *not* mean no effort. When my disciples told me that they had toiled all night and taken nothing, I did not fill the boat with fishes without effort on their part. No! My command stood. "Launch out into the deep and let down your nets for a draught."

Their lives were endangered, the ship nearly sank, the help of their fellows had to be summoned, and there were broken nets to mend. Any one of these troubles might have made them feel my help was not for them. And yet as they sat on the shore and mended those nets, they would see my love and care.

Man rises by effort.

The man who reaches the mountain height by the help of train or car has learned no climber's lesson. But remember this does not mean no guide—this does not mean that my Spirit is not supplying wisdom and strength. How often, when sometimes you little know it, do I go before you to prepare the way, to soften a heart here, to overrule there.

Bless Your Enemies   April 25

Say often, "God bless . . . ," of any whom you find in disharmony with you, or whom you desire to help. Say it, willing that showers of blessings and joy and success may fall upon them.

Leave to me the necessary correcting or training; *you* must only desire joy and blessing for them. At present your prayers are that they should be taught and corrected.

Oh! If my children would leave my work to me and occupy themselves with the task I give them. Love, love, love. Love will break down all your difficulties. Love will build up all your successes.

God the destroyer of evil, God the creator of good—is love. To love one another is to use God in your life. To use God in your life is to bring into manifestation all harmony, beauty, joy, and happiness.

I Make the Opportunities   April 26

Never doubt. Have no fear. Watch the faintest tremor of fear, and stop all work, everything, and rest before me until you are joyful and strong again.

Deal in the same way with all tired feelings. I was weary too, when on earth, and I separated myself from my disciples, and sat and rested on the well. Rested—and then it was that the Samaritan woman was helped.

Times of withdrawal for rest always precede fresh miracle-working. Learn of me. To accept the limitations of human flesh is to be subject, except as far as sin is concerned, to the same conditions as man.

I had to teach renewal of Spirit—force, rest of body to my disciples. Then, as your example, I lay with my Head on a pillow, asleep in the boat. It was not, as they thought, indifference. They cried, "Master, carest Thou not that we perish?" and I had to teach them that ceaseless activity was no part of my Father's plan.

When Paul said, "I can do all things through Christ who strengthens me," he did not mean that he was to do all things and then rely on me to find strength. he meant that for all I told him to do he could rely on my supplying the strength.

My work in the world has been hindered by work, work, work. Many a tireless, nervous body has driven a spirit. The spirit should be the master always, and just simply and naturally use the body as need should arise. Rest in me.

Do not *seek* to work for me. Never make opportunities. Live with me and for me. I do the work and I make the opportunities.

SEEING CHRIST   APRIL 27

I am beside you. Can you not feel my presence? Contact with me is not gained by the senses. Spirit-consciousness replaces sight.

When man sees me with his human sight it does not mean of necessity that his spiritual perception is greater. *Nay, rather that for that soul I have to span the physical and the spiritual with a spiritual vision clear to human eyes.*

Remember this to cheer my disciples who have never seen me, and yet have had a clear spiritual consciousness of me.

THE ROUNDABOUT WAY   APRIL 28

Through briars, through waste places, through glades, up mountain heights, down into valleys, I lead. But ever with the leadership goes the helping hand.

Glorious to follow where your master goes. But remember that the varied path does not always mean that *you* need the varied training.

We are seeking lost sheep—we are bringing the kingdom into places where it has not been known before. So realize that you are joining me on my quest—my undying quest, tracking down souls.

I am not choosing ways that will fret and tire—just to fret and tire; we are out to save. *You* may not always see the soul we seek. I know.

DISHARMONY   APRIL 29

Seek and ye shall find. Shall find that inner knowledge that makes the problems of life plain.

The difficulties of life are caused by disharmony in the individual. There is no discord in my kingdom, only a something unconquered in my disciples. The rule of my kingdom is perfect order, perfect harmony, perfect supply, perfect love, perfect honesty, perfect obedience—all power, all conquest, all success.

But so often my servants lack power, conquest, success, supply, harmony, and think I fail in my promises because these are not manifested in their lives.

These are but the outward manifestations that result from the obedience, honesty, order, love—and they come, not in answer to urgent prayer, but naturally as light results from a lighted candle.

SPRINGTIME   APRIL 30

Rejoice in the springtime of the year. Let there be springtime in your hearts. The full time of fruit is not yet but there is the promise of the blossom.

Know surely that your lives too are full of glad promise. Such blessings are to be yours. Such joys, such wonders.

All is indeed well. Live in my Sunshine and my love.

MAY

DELAY IS NOT DENIAL   MAY 1

Read the lessons of divine control in nature's laws.

Nature is but the expression of eternal thought in time. Study the outward form—grasp the eternal thought, and if you can read the thoughts of the Father, then indeed you know him.

Leave me out of nothing. Love all my ways with you. Know indeed that "All is well." Delay is but the wonderful and all-loving restraint of your Father—not reluctance, not desire to deny—but the divine control of a Father who can scarcely brook the delay.

Delay has to be—sometimes. Your lives are so linked up with those of others, so bound by circumstances that to let your desire have instant fulfillment might in many cases cause another, as earnest prayer, to go unanswered.

But think for a moment of the love and thoughtful care that seeks to harmonize and reconcile all your desires and longings and prayers.

Delay is not denial—not even withholding. It is the opportunity for God to work out your problems and accomplish your desires in the most wonderful way possible for you.

Oh! Children, trust me. Remember that your Maker is also your Servant, quick to fulfill, quick to achieve, faithful in accomplishment. Yes. All is well.

Souls That Smile — May 2

To conquer adverse circumstances, conquer yourselves. The answer to the desire of my disciples to follow me was "Be ye therefore perfect even as your Father who is in heaven is perfect."

To accomplish much, be much. In all cases the *doing*, to be well-doing, must be the mere unconscious expression of the *being*.

Fear not, fear not, all is well. Let the day be full of little prayers to me, little turnings towards me. The smiles of the soul at one it loves.

Men call the Father the first cause. Yes! See him as the first cause of every warm ray, every color in the sunset, every gleam on the water, every beautiful flower, every planned pleasure.

Kill Self Now — May 3

Self dethroned—that is the lesson, but in its place put love for me, knowledge of me.

Self, not only dethroned, but dead. A dead self is not an imprisoned self. An imprisoned self is more potent to harm. In all training—in mine of you, and in yours of others—let self die.

But for each blow to the life of self you must at the same time embrace and hold fast the new life, life with me.

It is not a dead self that men have to fear, but a thwarted, captive, imprisoned self. That self is infinitely more self-centered than the self allowed full play. But to you, my children, I teach a higher science-law than even freedom of the self. I teach death to the self. No repressions, just death. Petty self life exchanged for divine life.

And now I can make more clear to you what I would say about forgiveness of injuries. It is one of my commands that as you seek my forgiveness, so you must forgive.

But what you do not see is that you, the self in you, can never forgive injuries. The very thought of them means self in the foreground, then the injury, instead of appearing less, appears greater.

No, my children, as all true love is *of* God, and is God, so all true forgiveness is of God and is God. The self cannot forgive. Kill self.

Cease trying to forgive those who fretted or wronged you. It is a mistake to think about it. Aim at killing the self now—in your daily life, and then, and not until then, you will find there is nothing that even remembers injury, because the only one injured, the self, is dead.

As long as it recurs to your mind you deceive yourself if you think it forgiven. Forgiving injuries can be one way of feeding a self-life.

Many deceive themselves in this.

SHARE WITH ME   MAY 4

Delight in my love. Try to live in the rapture of the kingdom.

Claim big things. Claim great things. Claim joy and peace and freedom from care. Joy in me.

I am your Lord, your Creator. Remember too that I am the same yesterday, today, and forever. Your Creator, when my thought about the world called it into being—your Creator as much, too, today, when I can, by loving thought for you, call into being all you need on the material plane.

Joy in me, trust in me, share all life with me, see me in everything, rejoice in me. Share all with me as a child shares its pains and cuts and griefs and newfound treasures and joys and little work with its mother.

And give me the joy of sharing all with you.

LET ME CHOOSE   MAY 5

My loved ones. Yes, with the heart, not the head, men should think of me, and then worship would be instinctive.

Breathe in my very Spirit in pure air and fervent desire.

Keep the eye of your spirit ever upon me, the window of your soul open towards me. You have ever to know that all things are yours— that what is lovely I delight to give you.

Empty your mind of all that limits. Whatever is beautiful you can have. Leave more and more the choice to me. You will have no regrets.

SUBLIME AUDACITY   MAY 6

The way is long and weary. It is a weary world. So many today are weary. "Come unto me and I will give you rest."

My children, who range yourselves under my flag, you must see that on it are inscribed those words "The Son of Man."

Whatever the world is feeling, I must feel, I—the Son of Man. You are my followers—so the weariness of man today must be shared by you—the weary and heavy-laden must come to *you,* and find that rest that you found in me.

My children, my followers must be prepared not to sit on my right hand and on my left, but to drink of the cup that I drink of.

Poor world—teach it that there is only one cure for all its ills— union with me. Dare to suffer, dare to conquer, be filled with my sublime audacity. Remember that. Claim the unclaimable.

Just what the world would think impossible can always be yours. Remember, my children, sublime audacity.

AGAINST THE TIDE   MAY 7

The oarsman, trusting in me, does not lean on his oars and drift with the tide, trusting to the current.

Nay, more often—once I have shown the way—it is against the tide you must direct all your effort. And even when difficulties come, it is by your effort that they will be surmounted. But always strength and the joy in the doing you can have through me.

My fishermen-disciples did not find the fishes ready on the shore in their nets. I take man's effort and bless that. I need man's effort— he needs my blessing. This partnership it is that means success.

THE REST OF GOD   MAY 8

I lead you. The way is clear. Go forward unafraid. I am beside you. Listen, listen, listen to my voice. My hand is controlling all.

Remember that I can work through you better when you are at rest. Go very slowly, very quietly from one duty to the next—taking time to rest and pray between.

Do not be too busy. Take all in order as I say. The rest of God is in a realm beyond all man's activities. Venture there often, and you will indeed find peace and joy.

All work that results from resting with God is miracle-work. Claim the power to work miracles, both of you.

Know that you can do all things through Christ who strengthens you. Nay, more, know that you can do all things through Christ who rests you.

HARMONY WITHIN   MAY 9

Follow my guidance. Be afraid to venture on your own as a child fears to leave its mother's side. Doubt of your own wisdom, and reliance on mine will teach you humility.

Humility is not the belittling of the self. It is forgetting the self. Nay more, forgetting the self, because you are remembering me.

You must not expect to live in a world where all is harmony. You must not expect to live where others are in unbroken accord with you. It is your task to maintain your own heart peace in adverse circumstances. Harmony is always yours when you strain your ear to catch heaven's music.

Doubt always your power or wisdom to put things right, ask me to right all as you leave it to me and go on your way loving and laughing. I am wisdom. Only my wisdom can rightly decide anything—settle any problem. So rely on me. All is well.

CALM—NOT SPEED   MAY 10

In quietness and in confidence shall be your strength. (Isa. xxx. 15)

All agitation is destructive of good. All calm is constructive of good, and at the same time destructive of evil.

When man wants evil destroyed so often he rushes to action. It is wrong. First be still and know that I am God. Then act only as I tell you. Always calm with God. Calm is trust in action. Only trust, perfect trust can keep one calm.

Never be afraid of any circumstances or difficulties that help you to cultivate this calm. As the world, to attain, has to learn speed, you, to attain, have to learn calm. All great work for me is done first in the individual soul of the worker.

THE DIVINE THIRD   MAY 11

When I have led you through these storms there will be other words for you, other messages—other guidance.

So deep is your friendship and so great your desire to love and follow and serve me that soon, when this time of difficulty is over, to be alone together will always mean to be shut in with me.

There are few friendships in the world like that and yet I taught, when on earth, as I have taught you both, the power of the *two together.*

And now tonight I have more to say to you. I say that the time is coming, is even now here, when those who visit you two together will know that I am the divine Third in your friendship.

THRILL OF PROTECTION   MAY 12

Turn out all thoughts of doubt and of trouble. Never tolerate them for one second. Bar the windows and doors of your souls against them as you would bar your home against a thief who would steal in to take your treasures.

What greater treasures can you have than peace and rest and joy? And these are all stolen from you by doubt and fear and despair.

Face each day with love and laughter. Face the storm.

Joy, peace, love, my great gifts. Follow me to find all three. I want you to feel the thrill of protection and safety now. Any soul can feel this in a harbor, but real joy and victory come to those alone who sense these when they ride a storm.

Say "all is well." Say it not as a vain repetition. Use it as you use a healing balm for cut or wound, until the poison is drawn out; *then,* until the sore is healed; *then* until the thrill of fresh life floods your being.

All is well.

NEVER JUDGE   MAY 13

What joy follows self-conquest! You cannot conquer and control others, either of you, until you have completely conquered yourself.

Can you see yourselves absolutely unmoved? Think of me before the mocking soldiers, being struck, spat upon, and answering never a word—*never a word.* Try to see that as divine power. Remember by that power of perfect silence, perfect self-control, you can alone prove your right to govern.

Never judge. The heart of man is so delicate, so complex, only its Maker can know it. Each heart is so different, actuated by different motives, controlled by different circumstances, influenced by different sufferings.

How can one judge of another? Leave to me the unraveling of the puzzles of life. Leave to me the teaching of understanding. Bring each heart to me, its Maker, and leave it with me. Secure in the certainty that all that is wrong I can set right.

THE LOVE OF A LOVER   MAY 14

Remember that a loving master delights in the intimacy of demands made, as much as he desires his followers and friends to delight in the tender intimacy of *his* demands.

The wonder of family life is expressed in the freedom with which a child makes demands and claims, quite as much as in the loving demands the parent makes upon all the love and joy of the children. Only as the result of frequent converse with me, of much prayer to me, of listening to and obedience to my behests comes that intimacy that makes my followers dare to approach me as friend to friend.

Yield in all things to my tender insistence but remember I yield too to yours. Ask not only the big things I have told you, but ask the little tender signs of love. Remember that I came as the world's great lover. Never think of my love as only a tender compassion and forgiveness. It is that, but it is also the love of a lover, who shows his love by countless words and actions and by tender thought.

In each of you too, remember there is God. That God I reverence and submit to, though I and my Father are one. So as man grows more and more like my Father in heaven I bring to our friendship a reverent, tender love. I see as no man can see the God in you.

It is always given to man to see in his fellow man those aspirations and qualities he himself possesses. So only I, being really God, can recognize the God in man. Remember this, too, in your relation to others.

Your motives and aspirations can only be understood by those who have attained the same spiritual level. So do not vainly, foolishly, expect from others understanding. Do not misjudge them for not giving it. Yours is a foreign language to them.

FIRST THE SPIRITUAL   **MAY 15**

What can I say to you? Your heart is torn. Then remember "he bindeth up the broken hearts." Just feel the tenderness of my hands as I bind up your wounds.

You are very privileged both of you. I share my plans and secrets with you and make known to you my purposes, while so many have to grope on.

Try to rest on these words "Seek ye first the kingdom of God and his righteousness and all these things shall be added unto you." Then strive not for *them* but, untiringly, for the things of my kingdom.

It is so strange to you mortals, you would think the material things first and then grow into the knowledge of spiritual things. Not so in my kingdom. It is spiritual things first and then material. So to attain the material redouble your efforts to acquire the spiritual.

PRAY AND PRAISE   **MAY 16**

I will be much entreated because I know that only in that earnest supplication, and the calm trust that results, does man learn strength and gain peace. Therefore I have laid that incessant, persistent pleading as a duty upon my disciples.

Never weary in prayer. When one day man sees how marvelously his prayer has been answered, then he will deeply, so deeply, regret that he prayed so little.

Prayer changes all. Prayer recreates. Prayer is irresistible. So pray, literally without ceasing.

Pray until you almost cease to pray, because trust has become so rock-like, and then pray on because it has become so much a habit that you cannot resist it.

And always pray until Prayer merges into praise. That is the only note on which true prayer should end. It is the love and laughter of your attitude towards man interpreted in the pray and praise of your attitude towards God.

SORROW TO JOY   MAY 17

"Sorrow may endure for a night, but joy cometh in the morning."

My bravest are those who can anticipate the morning and feel in the night of sorrow that underlying joy that tells of confident expectations of the morning.

NEW AND VITAL POWER   MAY 18

"Look unto me and be ye saved all the ends of the earth." Not for merit was salvation, the promise was to all who looked.

To look is surely within the power of everyone. One look suffices. salvation follows.

Look and you are saved from despair. Look and you are saved from care. Look and you are saved from worry. Look, and into you there flows a peace beyond all understanding—a power new and vital, a joy wonderful indeed.

Look and keep looking. Doubt flees, joy reigns and hope conquers.

Life, eternal life, is yours—revitalizing, renewing.

RESCUED AND GUIDED   MAY 19

Rest knowing all is so safe in my hands. Rest is Trust. Ceaseless activity is distrust. Without the knowledge that I am working for you, you do not rest. Inaction then would be the outcome of despair.

"My hand is not shortened that it cannot save." Know that, repeat it, rely on it, welcome the knowledge, delight in it. Such a truth is as a hope flung to a drowning man. Every repetition of it is one pull nearer shore and safety.

Let that illustration teach you a great truth. Lay hold of the truth, pray it, affirm it, hold onto the rope. How foolish are your attempts to save yourself, one hand on the rope, and one making efforts to swim ashore! You may relinquish your hold of the rope and hinder the rescuer—who has to act with the greater caution lest he lose you.

The storms and tempests are not all of life. The Psalmist who said "All Thy waves and Thy billow's are gone over me" wrote also "he brought me up also out of a horrible pit, out of the miry clay, and set my feet upon a rock and established my goings."

Meditate upon that wonder—truth, the three steps—safety, security, guidance.

1. "He brought me up also out of a horrible pit"—*Safety.*
2. "He set my feet upon a rock"—*Security.*
3. "He established my goings"—*Guidance.*

Number 3 is the final stage when the saved soul trusts me so entirely it seeks no more its own way but leaves all future plans to me its rescuer.

WIN ME—WIN ALL   MAY 20

You will conquer. The conquering spirit is never crushed. Keep a brave and trusting heart. Face all your difficulties in the spirit of Conquest.

Rise to greater heights than you have known before. Remember where I am is victory. Forces of evil, within and without you, flee at my presence.

Win *me* and all is won. *All.*

FLING IT AT MY FEET   MAY 21

To see me you must bring me your cares and show me your heart of Trust. Then, as you leave your cares, you become conscious of my presence.

This consciousness persisted in brings its reward of me. Through a mist of care no man may see my face. Only when the burden is flung at my Feet do you pass on to consciousness and spiritual sight.

Remember obedience, obedience, obedience—the straight and narrow way into the kingdom. Not of you must it be said, even in lovingly tender reproach—"Why call ye me 'Lord, Lord' and do not the things that I say."

Character is chiseled into beauty by the daily discipline and daily duties done. For, in many ways, my disciples must work out their own salvation, though this is not possible without my strength and help, and without converse with me.

Even for the spiritual life the training is different for different spirits. The man who would fain live a life of prayer and meditation is thrust into the busy ways of life, and the busy man is bidden to rest and wait patiently for me. O joy, O rest, and in the busy ways be ever at peace.

COMMAND YOUR LORD   MAY 22

Lord, I claim Thy help.

Yes! Claim, be constantly claiming. There is a trust that waits long, and a trust that brooks no delay—that once convinced of the right of a course, once sure of God's guidance, says with all the persistence of a child, *"now."* "Make no long tarrying, oh, my God."

You are no longer servants but friends. A friend can command his friend—can know that all the friend, the true friend, has is his by right. That does not mean an idle living at the expense of a friend, but the claiming the friend's means: name, time, all that he has, when your supply is exhausted.

Friendship—true friendship, implies the right to appropriate. And in God's service is perfect freedom. Heirs of God—you are joint heirs with me in the inheritance. We share the Father's property. You have the same right to use and claim as I have. Use your right. A beggar supplicates. A son, a daughter, appropriates.

Small wonder when I see my children sitting before my house supplicating and waiting—that I leave them there until they realize how foolish such action, when they have only to walk into their home and take.

This cannot be the attitude of all. There must be first a definite realization of Sonship.

LITTLE FRETS   MAY 23

Your lack of control is not due to the *big* burdens, but to your permitting the *little* frets and cares and burdens to accumulate.

If anything vex you, deal with that and get that righted with me before you allow yourself to speak to, or meet anybody, or to undertake any new duty.

Look upon yourself more as performing my errands and coming back quickly to me to tell me that message is delivered, that task done.

Then with no feeling of responsibility as to result (your only responsibility was to see the duty done) go out again, rejoicing at still more to do for my sake.

ABUNDANCE   MAY 24

How unseeing the world goes on! How unknowing of your heartaches and troubles, your battles won, your conquests, your difficulties.

But be thankful, both of you, that there is One who knows, One who marks every crisis, every effort, every heartache.

For you both, who are not idle hearers, *you* must know that every troubled soul I tell you of, is one for you to help. You must help all you can. You do not help enough. As you help, help will flow back and your circle of helpfulness will widen more and more, ever more and more.

Just feel that you are two of my disciples, present at the feeding of the five thousand, and that to you I hand out the food, and you pass it on, and ever more and more. You can always say with so few loaves and fishes, "We have only enough for our own needs." It was not only my blessing, but the passing-on of the disciples that worked the miracle.

Get a feeling of bounteous giving into your beings. They were "all filled." There was a supply over.

I give with a large hand and heart. Note the draught of fishes. The net broke, the boat began to sink with the lavishness of my gift. Lose sight of all limitations.

Abundance is God's supply. Turn out all limited thoughts. Receive *showers* and in your turn—*shower.*

ACCOMPLISH ANYTHING   MAY 25

There will be no limit to what you can accomplish. Realize that. Never relinquish any task or give up the thought of any task because it seems beyond your power, only if you see it is not my will for you. This I command you.

Think of the tiny snowdrop-shoot in the hard ground. No certainty even that when it has forced its weary way up, sunlight and warmth will greet it.

What a task beyond its power that must seem. But the inner urge of life within the seed compelling it, it carries out that task. The kingdom of heaven is like unto this.

CLAIM MORE   MAY 26

You are doing your claiming as I have said, and soon you will see the result. You cannot do this long without it being seen in the material. It is an undying law.

You are at present children practicing a new lesson. Practice—practice—soon you will be able to do it so readily.

You see others manifesting so easily, so readily demonstrating my power. But you have not seen the discipline that went before. Discipline absolutely necessary before this power is given to my disciples. It is a further initiation.

You are feeling you have learnt so much that life cannot be a failure. That is right, but others have to wait to see the outward manifestation in your lives before they realize this spiritual truth.

ROOTS AND FRUITS   MAY 27

Remember the lesson of the *seed* too in its sending a shoot down so that it may be rooted and grounded, while at the same time it sends a shoot up to be the plant and flower that shall gladden the world.

The two growths are necessary. Without the strong root it would soon wither, as much activity fails for lack of growth in me, The higher the growth up, the deeper must be the enrooting.

Many forget this and thus their work ceases to be permanent for me. Beware of the leaves and flowers without the strong root.

TEST YOUR LOVE   MAY 28

A great love knows that in every difficulty, every trial, every failure, the presence of the loved one suffices. Test your love for me by this.

Just to be with me, just to know I am beside you—does that bring you joy and peace? If not then your love for me, and your realization of my love, are at fault.

Then, if this be so, pray for more love.

FORGET   MAY 29

Regret nothing. Not even the sins and failures. When a man views
earth's wonders from some mountain height he does not spend his
time in dwelling on the stones and stumbles, the faints and failures,
that marked his upward path.

So with you. Breathe in the rich blessings of each new day—forget
all that lies behind you.

Man is so made that he can carry the weight of twenty-four hours—
no more. Directly he weighs down with the years behind, and the days
ahead, his back breaks. I have promised to help you with the burden
of today only, the past I have taken from you and if you, foolish hearts,
choose to gather again that burden and bear it, then, indeed, you
mock me to expect me to share it.

For weal or woe each day is ended. What remains to be lived, the
coming twenty-four hours, you must face as you awake.

A man on a march on earth carries only what he needs for that
march. Would you pity him if you saw him bearing too the overwhelming weight of the worn-out shoes and uniforms of past marches and
years? And yet, in the mental and spiritual life, man does these things.
Small wonder my poor world is heartsick and weary.

Not so must *you* act.

THE DEVIL'S DEATH KNELL   MAY 30

Our Lord, we praise Thee.

Praise is the devil's death knell. Resignation, acceptance of my will,
obedience to it, have not the power to vanquish evil that praise has.

The joyful heart is my best weapon against all evil. Oh! Pray
and praise.

You are learning your lesson. You are being led out into a large
place. Go with songs of rejoicing. Rejoice evermore. Happy indeed if
each day has its thrill of joy.

Talk to me more during the day. Look up into my face—a look of
love, a feeling of security, a thrill of joy at the sense of the nearness
of my presence—these are your best prayers.

Let these smooth the day's work, then fear will vanish, and fear is the grim figure that turns aside success.

PRAYER WITHOUT WORDS   MAY 31

Lord, hear us, we pray.

Hear and I answer. Spend much time in prayer. Prayer is of many kinds, but of whatever kind, prayer is the linking up of the soul and mind and heart to God.

So that if it is only a glance of faith, a look or word of love, or confidence, and no supplication is expressed, it yet follows that supply and all necessary are secured.

Because the soul, being linked to God, united to him, receives in and through him all things. And the soul, when in human form, needs too the things belonging to its habitation.

JUNE

COMPANIONSHIP   JUNE 1

The way of the soul's transformation is the way of divine companionship.

Not so much the asking me to make you this or that but the living with me, thinking of me, talking to me—thus you grow like me.

Love me. Rest in me.

Joy in me.

MY IMAGE   JUNE 2

My Lord and my God, we praise Thee, we bless Thee, we worship Thee. Make us like Thee.

You are willing to drink of the cup that I drink of—the wine of sorrow and disappointment.

You are mine and will grow both of you more and more like me, your master.

True it is today as it was in the days of Moses that no man can see my face and live.

The self, the original *Man*, shrivels up and dies, and upon the soul becomes stamped my image.

EJECT SIN WITH LOVE   JUNE 3

Our Lord, we love and praise Thee. Thou art our joy and our exceeding great reward.

Remember that love is the power which transforms the world. Love not only of me, love not only of the few dear to you, but love of all—of the publicans—the sinners—the harlots—*love*.

It is the only weapon with which sin can be driven out. Drive sin out with love.

Drive fear and depression and despair and a sense of failure out with praise.

Praise is the acknowledgment of that which I have sent you. Few men would send a further gift of payment until they had received the acknowledgment of the previous one. So praise, acknowledging, as it does, that my gift and blessing leaves the way open for me to shower yet more on the thankful heart.

Learn as a child learns to say "Thank you" as a courtesy, with perhaps no real sense of gratitude at all. Do this until at last a thrill of joy, of thankful awe, will accompany the spoken word.

Do not expect for yourselves feeling that you know others have or have had. Just go on along the arid way of obedience, and persistence will be rewarded as you come to the spring, the glad spring of Water.

Oh, joy in me, and, as far as in you lies, shed joy on all around.

DIVINE PATIENCE   JUNE 4

Lord, make us like Thee. Mold us into Thy likeness.

Molding, my children, means cutting and chiseling. It means sacrifice of the personal to conform to type. It is not only my work but yours.

The swift recognition of the selfish in your desires and motives, actions, words and thoughts, and the instant appeal to me for help to eradicate that.

It is a work that requires cooperation—mine and yours. It is a work that brings much sense of failure and discouragement too, at times, because, as the work proceeds, you see more and more clearly all that yet remains to be done.

Shortcomings you had hardly recognized or at least for which you had had no sense of sorrow, now cause you trouble and dismay.

Courage. That is in itself a sign of progress.

Patience, not only with others, but, each of you, with herself.

As you see the slow progress upward made by you, in spite of your longing and struggle, you will gain a divine patience with others whose imperfections trouble you.

So on and up. Forward. Patience—perseverance—struggle. Remember that I am beside you, your captain and your helper. So tender, so patient, so strong.

Yes, we cooperate and as I share your troubles, failures, difficulties, heartaches, so, as my friends, you share my patience, and my strength—beloved.

THAT TENDER VOICE   JUNE 5

Very quietly I speak. Listen to my voice. Never heed the voices of the world—only the tender divine voice.

Listen and you will never be disappointed. Listen, and anxious thoughts and tired nerves will become rested. The voice divine—not so much in strength as in tenderness. Not so much in power as in restfulness.

But the tenderness and the restfulness will heal your scars and make you strong, and then it must be your task to let all your power be my power. Man's little power is as clay beside the granite rock of my power.

You are my great care. Never feel at the mercy of the world. My angels guard you day and night and nothing can harm you. You would indeed thank me if you knew the darts of fret and evil they turn from you.

Thank me indeed for dangers unknown—unseen—but averted.

HOW MEN SEE ME   JUNE 6

I came to help a world. And according to the varying needs of each so does each man see me.

It is not necessary that you see me as others see me—the world, even the church, my disciples, my followers, but it is necessary that *you* see me, each of you, as supplying all that *you* personally need.

The weak need my strength. The strong need my tenderness. The tempted and fallen need my salvation. The righteous need my pity for sinners. The lonely need a friend, The fighters need a leader.

No *man* could be all these to men—only a God could be. In each of these relations of mine to man you must see the God. The God-friend, the God-leader, the God-Savior.

TRUE BEAUTY   JUNE 7

Incline your ear, and come unto me: hear and your soul shall live.
(Isa. lv. 3)

Not only live but grow in grace and power and beauty—the true beauty, the beauty of holiness.

Reach ever forward after the things of my kingdom.

In the animal world the very form of an animal alters to enable it to reach that upon which it delights to feed.

So reaching after the treasures of my kingdom your whole nature becomes changed, so that you can best enjoy and receive the wonders of that kingdom.

Dwell on these truths.

THE ONLY WAY   JUNE 8

Down through the ages my power alone has kept millions of souls brave and true and strong who else would have fallen by the way.

The faith has been kept alive and handed down, not by the dwellers in ease, but by those who struggled and suffered and died for me.

This life is not for the body, it is for the soul, and man too often chooses the way of life that best suits the body. Not the way that best suits the soul. And I permit only what best suits the soul.

Accept this and a wonderful molding is the result, reject it and my purpose is frustrated, your best prayer unanswered, progress (spiritual progress) delayed, trouble and grief stored up.

Try, each of you, to picture your soul as a third, being trained by us—by you and me—and then you will share, and rejoice in sharing, in the discipline and training.

Stand apart from your soul with me and welcome training—rejoice at progress.

AN OBSTACLE RACE   JUNE 9

Rise above your fears and fancies into my joy. It will suffice to heal all your sores and wounds. Forget all sense of failure and shortcomings, all the painful jolts and jars, and trust me, love me, call upon me.

Your discipleship is an obstacle race. "So run that ye may obtain." Obtain not only your hearts' desires, but obtain me—your souls' joy and Haven.

What would you think of the runner who threw himself on the ground in despondency at his first hurdle?

Over, and on and up, I am your leader and your goal.

THE DAY OF TROUBLE   JUNE 10

Offer unto me the sacrifice of thanksgiving and pay your vows to the Most High, and then call upon me in the day of trouble and I will deliver you.

To praise and thank and steadily fulfill your promises (vows) to me are then, as it were, the placing of coin in my Bank, upon which, in your time of need, you can draw with confidence and certainty. Remember that.

The world wonders when it sees the man who can so unexpectedly draw large and unsuspected sums from his bank for his own need, that of a friend or for some charity.

But what the world has not seen are the countless small sums paid into that bank, earned by faithful work in many ways.

And so in my kingdom. The world sees the man of faith make a sudden demand upon me, upon my stores, and lo! That demand is met.

The world thinks the man has magic power—no! The world does not see that the man has been paying in, in thanks and praise, promises fulfilled—faithfully, steadily.

So with you, my children. "Offer to God the sacrifice of thanksgiving and pay your vows to the Most High and call upon me in the day of trouble and I will deliver you."

This is a promise for the seemingly dull days of little happenings, and a cheer for you, my children. When you seem not able to do big things you can be storing your little acts and words of faithfulness in my great storehouse, ready for the day of your big demand.

MY MARK! JUNE 11

O Lord, we thank Thee for Thy great gift of peace.

That is the peace that only I can give in the midst of a restless world and surrounded by trouble and difficulty. To know that peace is to have received the stamp of the kingdom—the mark of the Lord Jesus Christ. My mark.

When you have learned that peace you are fit to judge of true values, the values of the kingdom, and the values of all the world has to offer.

That peace is loving faith at rest.

HOUSE ON A ROCK JUNE 12

Be watchful to hear my voice and instantly to obey. Obedience is your great sign of faith. "Why call ye me Lord, Lord, and do not the things that I say" was my word when on earth to the many who followed and heard, but did not do.

I likened the man who heard and did not do to the man who built his house on the sand. In times of storm and trouble he is overthrown, his house falls.

I likened the man who obeyed me implicitly to the man who built his house upon a rock. In times of storm he is steadfast, immovable.

Do not feel that by this I mean only the keeping of my Commandments, even the living my Sermon on the Mount. I mean more than that to those who know me intimately. I mean the following, in all, the Inner guiding that I give, the little injunctions I speak to each individual soul, the wish I express—and desire to have carried out.

The secure, steadfast, immovable life of my disciples, the rock home, is not built at a wish, in a moment, but is laid, stone by stone, foundations, walls, roof, by the acts of obedience, the daily following out of my wishes, the loving doing of my will.

"He that heareth these sayings of mine and doeth them is like unto a man who built his house upon a rock, and the rain descended and the floods came, and the winds blew and beat upon that house and it fell not, for it was founded upon a rock."

And it is in that rock-home, manmade but divinely inspired—the house of obedience—the truest expression of a disciple's adoration and worship—it is *there* I come to dwell with my loved one.

Am I not giving you work, hope? Work for the grey days? Just little plain bricks of duties done and my wishes carried out. All strengthening you and making of your character that steadfast, immovable Christian character of which my servant Paul spoke and which he urged his followers to have.

GOD-INSPIRED   JUNE 13

You have entered now upon a mountain climb. Steep steps lead upward, but your power to help others will be truly marvelous.

Not alone will you arise. All towards whom you now send loving, pitying thoughts will be helped upward by you.

Looking to me all your thoughts are God-inspired. Act on them and you will be led on. They are not your own impulses but the movement of my Spirit and, obeyed, will bring the answer to your prayers.

Love and Trust. Let no unkind thoughts of any dwell in your hearts, then I can act with all my Spirit—power, with nothing to hinder.

FACE TODAY WITH ME   JUNE 14

Our Lord and our God. Make us all thou wouldst have us.

It is not circumstances that need altering first, but yourselves, and then the conditions will naturally alter. Spare no effort to become all I would have you. Follow every leading. I am your only guide.

Endeavor to put from you every thought of trouble. Take each day, and with no backward look, face the day's problem with me, and seek my help and guidance as to what you can do.

Never look back and never leave until the morrow that on which you can get my guidance for today.

"Glory, Glory Dawneth"   June 15

I am planning for you. Wonderful are my ways beyond your knowledge.

Oh! Realize my Bounty and my Goodness more and more. The wonder of being led by me! The beauty of a guided life!

These will enter your consciousness more and more and bring you ever more and more joy.

You are very very nearly at the point when you shall ask what you will and it shall be done unto you.

You have entered upon a wonderful era—your lives are planned and blessed by me as never before.

You are overcoming. You are counting all things but loss if you can win me. And the promises to him that overcometh are truly wonderful, and will always be fulfilled.

Seek Me Early   June 16

Walk in my way and trust me. No evil can touch you. I am yours as truly as you are mine. Rest in that truth.

Rest, that is, cease all struggle. Gain a calm, strong confidence in that certainty. Do not only rest in me when the world's struggles prove too much and too many for you to bear or face alone. Rest in me when you need perfect understanding, when you need the consciousness of tender, loving friendship and intercourse.

The world, my poor world, flies to me when its difficulties are too great to be surmounted any other way, forgetting, or never realizing, that if, with the same eagerness, those hearts sought me merely for companionship and loving intercourse, many of the difficulties would not arise.

The circumstances, the life, the character would be so altered—so purified, that those same difficulties would not exist.

Seek me *early* that is the way to find me. *Early*, before I get crowded out by life's troubles, and difficulties and pleasures.

Dear Name   June 17

"Jesus." Say my name often. It was in my name Peter bade the lame man walk. "In the name of Jesus Christ of Nazareth arise and walk."

"Jesus." The very sounding of my name, in love and tenderness, drives away all evil. It is the word before which all the hosts of evil flee.

"Jesus." My name is the call for a life line to rescue you from temptation.

"Jesus." The name banishes loneliness—dispels gloom.

"Jesus." Summons help to conquer your faults.

I will set you on high because you have known my name.

Yes! My name—"Jesus." Use it more. Use it tenderly. Use it prayerfully. Use it powerfully.

WAIT   JUNE 18

The world has always seen service for me to be activity. Only those near to me have seen that a life apart, of prayer, may, and does so often, accomplish more than all the service man can offer me.

If man lived apart with me and only went out to serve at my direct command my Spirit could operate more and accomplish truly mighty things.

THE SUCCESS YOU COVET   JUNE 19

Follow the path of obedience. It leads to the throne of God. Your treasure, be it success necessary on the material plane, which will further the work of my kingdom, or the hidden spiritual wonders revealed by me to those only who diligently seek, this treasure lies at the end of the track.

From one point (a promise of mine or a command) to the next, you have to follow, till finally you reach the success you covet.

All *your* work for the moment is in the material plane and the spiritual is only to help the material. When your material goal is reached then the material will serve only to attain the spiritual.

MIRACLES AGAIN   JUNE 20

Wait to hear my will and then obey. At all costs obey.

Do not fear. I am a wall of protection around you. See this. To see this with the eyes of faith is to cause it to manifest in the material.

Remember I long to work miracles, as when on earth I wrought them, but the same condition holds good. I cannot do many mighty works because of unbelief.

So only in response to your belief can I do miracle-works now.

SEE AS I SEE   JUNE 21

O Lord, we praise Thee. Bless us, we beseech Thee.

I bless you. I promise you release. Joy in me. You shall be shielded from the storm.

Wonders have unfolded. Just to come before me and stay for a while in my presence—this must strengthen and help you.

Learn of me. The only way for so many in my poor world to keep calm, sane, is to have the mind which is in Jesus Christ. The mind which is in me.

That mind you can never obtain by reasoning, or by reading, but only by living with me and sharing my life.

Think much of me. Speak much of me. See others as I see them. Let nothing less satisfy you.

YOUR RED SEA   JUNE 22

Go forward fearlessly.

Do not think about the Red Sea that lies ahead.

Be very sure that when you come to it the waters will part and you will pass over to your Promised Land of freedom.

CLING TO ME   JUNE 23

Cling to me until the life from me—the divine life, by that very contact, flows into your being and revives your fainting spirit.

Become recharged. When weary, do as I did on earth—*Sit by the well. Rest.*

Rest and gain power and strength and the work too will come to you as it came to me.

Rest till every care-thought has gone, and then let the Tide of love and joy flow in.

WHEN GUIDANCE TARRIES   JUNE 24

As I prompt you—act. When you have no clear guidance, then go forward quietly along the path of duty I have set before you.

No fear, no panic, quietly doing your daily duty.

This attitude of faith will receive its reward, as surely as the acting upon my direct guidance.

Rejoice in the sense of security that is yours.

GOD'S FRIENDSHIP   JUNE 25

I am your friend. The companion of the dreary ways of life.

I rob those ways of their greyness and horror. I transform them. Even in earthly friendships the common way, the weary way, the steep way, may seem a way to heaven if the presence of some loved human friend transforms them.

Let the Sabbath calm enwrap your minds and hearts. Let it be a rest from the worry and fret of life, a halt by the busy highway when you seek some rest and shade.

Have you ever realized the wonder of the friendship you can have with me? Hare you ever thought what it means to be able to summon at will the God of the world?

Even with a privileged visitor to an earthly king there is the palace antechamber, and the time must be at the pleasure of the king.

But to my subjects I have given the right to enter my presence when they will, nay more they can summon me to bedside, to workshop—and I am there.

Could divine love do more? Your nearest earthly friend cannot be with you on the instant. Your Lord, your master, your divine friend—yes.

When men seek to worship me they think of the worlds I rule over, of creation, of mighty law and order—and then they feel the awe that precedes worship.

To you I say feel awe, feel the desire to worship me in wondering amazement. But think too of the mighty, tender, humble condescension of my friendship. Think of me in the little things of everyday life.

Do Not Rush   JUNE 26

Learn in the little daily things of life to delay action until you get
my guidance. . . .

So many lives lack poise. For in the momentous decisions and
the big things of life, they ask my help but into the small things they
rush alone.

By what you do in the small things those around you are most
often antagonized or attracted.

No Self-Reproach   JUNE 27

The eternal Arms shelter you. "Underneath are the Everlasting Arms."
This promise is to those who rise above the earth-life and seek to soar
higher, to the kingdom of heaven.

You must not feel the burden of your failure, Go on in faith, the
clouds will clear, and the way will lighten—the path becomes less
stony with every step you take. So run that you may *obtain*. A rigid
doing of the simple duties, and success will crown your efforts.

I had no words of reproach for any I healed. The man was whole
and free who had wrecked his physical being by sin—whose palsy
I healed.

The woman at the well was not overwhelmed by my "Thou hast
five husbands, he whom thou hast is not thy husband."

The woman taken in adultery was told "neither do I condemn
thee, go and sin no more." She was not told to bear the burden of the
consciousness of her sin. . . .

Remember now abideth these three, faith, hope and charity.
Faith is your attitude towards me. Charity your attitude towards your
fellow man but, as necessary, is hope, which is confidence in yourself to succeed.

Table of Delights   JUNE 28

It has not been in vain this training and teaching time. The time of
suppression, repression, depression is changed now into a time of glorious expression.

Life is flooded through and through with joy and Gladness. Indeed I have prepared a table of delights, a feast of all good things for you.

Indeed your cup runneth over and you can feel from the very depth of your heart. "Surely goodness and mercy shall follow us all the days of our lives and we shall dwell in the house of the Lord forever."

MY WILL—YOUR JOY   JUNE 29

Our Lord and our God. Lead us, we beseech Thee. Lead us and keep us.

You can never go beyond my love and care. Remember that. No evil can befall you. Circumstances I bless and use must be the right ones for you.

But I know always that the first step is to lay your will before me as an offering, ready that I shall do what is best, sure that, if you trust me, what I do for you will be best.

Your second step is to be sure, and to tell me so, that I am powerful enough to do everything ("The hearts of kings are in my rule and governance"), that no miracle is impossible with me ("With God all things are possible" and I and my Father are one).

Then leave all with me. Glad to leave all your affairs in a master hand. Sure of safety and protection. Remember *you* cannot see the future, *I* can.

You could not bear it. So only little by little can I reveal it to you. Accept my will and it will bring you joy.

UNDERSTAND THEM   JUNE 30

Take joy wherever you go. You have been much blessed. You are being much blessed.

Such stores of blessing are awaiting you in the months and years that lie ahead. Pass every blessing on.

Love can and does go round the world, passed on the God-currents from one to the other.

Shed a little sunshine in the heart of one, that one is cheered to pass it on, and so my vitalizing joy-giving message goes.

Be transmitters these days. Love and laugh. Cheer all. Love all.

Always seek to understand others and you cannot fail to love them.

See me in the dull, the uninteresting, the sinful, the critical, the miserable.

See me in the laughter of children and the sweetness of old age, in the courage of youth and the patience of man and womanhood.

JULY

ATTACK FEAR   JULY 1

Learn daily the sublime lesson of trust and calm in the midst of storm. Whatever of sorrow or difficulty the day may bring my tender command to you is still the same—*love and laugh.*

Love and laughter, not a sorrowful resignation, mark real acceptances of my will. Leave every soul the braver and happier for having met you. For children or youth, middle or old age, for sorrow, for sin, for all you may encounter in others, this should be your attitude. *Love* and *laugh.*

Do not fear. Remember how I faced the devil in the wilderness, and how I conquered with "the sword of the spirit which is the word of God." You too have your quick answer for every fear that evil may present—an answer of faith and confidence in me. Where possible say it aloud.

The spoken word has power. Look on every fear, not as a weakness on your part due to illness or worry, but as a very real temptation to be attacked and overthrown.

THE CHILD-SPIRIT   JULY 2

Does the way seem a stony one? Not one stone can impede your progress. Courage. Face the future, but *face* it only with a brave and happy heart. Do not seek to *see* it. You are robbing faith of her sublime sweetness if you do this.

Just know that all is well and that faith, not seeing, but believing, is the barque that will bear you to safety, over the stormy waters. "According to your faith be it unto you" was my injunction to those who sought healing of me.

If for wonder-working, if for healing, if for salvation faith was so necessary then the reason is clear why I urged that all who sought entrance to my kingdom must become as little children. Faith is the child-attitude.

Seek in every way to become childlike. Seek, seek, seek until you find, until the years have added to your nature that of the trusting child. Not only for its simple trust must you copy the child-spirit, but for its joy in life, its ready laughter, its lack of criticism, its desire to share all with all men. Ask much that you may become as little children, friendly and loving towards all—not critical, not fearful.

"Except ye become as little children ye cannot enter the kingdom of heaven."

SPIRITUAL FULLNESS   JULY 3

Our Lord, we love Thee and desire to live for Thee in all things.

My children, "Blessed are they that hunger and thirst after righteousness, for they shall be filled." That is satisfaction.

Only in that fullness of spiritual things can the heartsick and faint and weary be satisfied, healed and rested "Lord," we cry, "to whom shall we go but to Thee." "Thou preparest a table before us." Bread of life, food from heaven.

How few realize that the feeding of the four thousand and the five thousand was in each case but an illustration of the way in which I should one day be the food of my people.

Think of the wonder of revelation still to be seen by those who live with me. All these hundreds of years, and much of what I said and did is still mystery, much of my life on earth is still spiritually unexplored country. Only to the simple and the loving heart that walks with me can these things be revealed. I have carefully hidden these things from the wise and prudent and have revealed them unto babes.

Do not weigh your spirits down with the sins and sorrows of the world. Only a Christ can do that and live. Look for the loving, the true, the kindly, the brave in the many all around you.

FRIEND OF MINE   JULY 4

What man calls conversion is often only the discovery of the great friend. What man calls religion is the knowledge of the great friend. What man calls holiness is the imitation of the great friend.

Perfection, that perfection I enjoined on all, the being perfect as your Father in heaven is perfect, is the being like the great friend and in turn becoming to others a great friend too.

I am your friend. Think again of all that means—friend and Savior. A friend is ready to help, anticipating every want, hand outstretched to help and encourage, or to ward off danger, voice of tenderness to soothe tired nerves and speak peace to restlessness and fear.

Think of what, to you, your friend is and then from that, try to see a little of what the Perfect friend, the tireless, selfless, all-conquering, all miracle-working friend would be. *That* friend, and more even than your heart can imagine, that *friend* am I.

Were I to read my kingdom—my kingdom of the child hearts—the doctrines of your churches, so often there would be no response. But the simple rules I gave my followers are known, loved and lived by them all.

In all things seek simplicity.

YOU ARE INVINCIBLE   JULY 5

I am with you all the time controlling, blessing, and helping you. No man or woman can stand against my will for you. A whole world of men and women cannot do this—if you trust me and place your affairs in my hands.

To the passenger it may seem as if each wave would overwhelm the ship, or turn it aside from its course. The captain knows by experience that, in spite of wind and wave, he steers a straight course to the haven where he would be.

So trust me, the captain of your salvation.

RICHES   JULY 6

Never let yourselves think "we cannot afford this," or "shall never be able to do that." Say "the supply for it is not here yet, but it will come if we should have it. It *will* surely come."

Persevere in saying that and gradually a feeling of being plentifully supplied and of being surrounded by riches will possess you. That feeling is your faith claiming my supply, and according to your faith it shall be unto you.

But it is not the faith expressed in moments of prayer and exaltation I look for but the faith that lays immediately to rest the doubts of the day as they arise, that attacks and conquers the sense of limitation.

"Ask and ye shall receive."

PAINFUL PREPARATION   JULY 7

Help and peace and joy are here. Your courage will be rewarded.

Painful as this time is you will both one day see the reason of it, and see too that it was not cruel testing, but tender preparation for the wonderful lifework you are both to do.

Try to realize that your own prayers are being most wonderfully answered. Answered in a way that seems painful to you, but that just now is the only way.

Success in the temporal world would not satisfy you.

Great success, in both temporal and spiritual worlds, awaits you. I know you will see this had to be.

MY SECRET   JULY 8

You are being guided but remember that I said "I will guide thee with mine eye."

And my eye is my set purpose—my will.

To guide with my will is to bring all your desires into oneness with my will, my desires.

To make my will your only will. Then my will guides *you*.

WHY DOUBT?   JULY 9

Joy in me. Joy is infectious. Trust and pray. It is not sin for one who knows me only as God, as Creator, to doubt me, to question my love and purposes.

But for one who knows me as you do, as friend and Savior, and who knows the world's God as Father—for that one to doubt my purpose and saving power and tender love is wrong indeed.

EXPECT MANY MIRACLES   JULY 10

My guardianship is so wonderful.

Expect not one miracle but many.

Each day's happenings, if of my working, and under my control, are miracle-works.

GUARDIAN ANGELS   JULY 11

You are mine. Once I have set on you my stamp and seal of ownership all my Hosts throng to serve and protect you.

Remember that you are daughters of a king.

Try to picture a bodyguard of my servitors in the unseen waiting, longing, efficient, to do all that is necessary for your well-being.

Feel this as you go through the day. Feel this and all is well.

SAVIOR AND SAVIOR   .   JULY 12

If you believe it is my hand that has saved you, then you must believe that I am meaning to save you yet more, and to keep you in the way that you should go.

Even a human rescuer does not save a man from drowning only to place him in other deep and dangerous waters. But rather to place him on dry land—and more—there to restore him to animation and health, and to see him to his home.

From this parable learn what I your rescuer would do, and even more. Is the Lord's hand shortened that it cannot perform and cannot save?

My cry on the cross of "It is finished" is my Cry of salvation for a whole world.

I complete every task committed to me. So trust and be not afraid.

EXPECT THE GOOD   JULY 13

Can you get the expectant attitude of faith?

Not waiting for the next evil to befall you but awaiting with a child's joyful trust the next good in store?

TRUE SUCCESS   JULY 14

Our Lord, we thank Thee that Thou hast kept us.

Rejoice indeed that you see my hand in all the happenings and the keepings of the day. Protected, the Israelites crossed the Red Sea; so are you protected in all things.

Rely on this and go forward. You have now entered upon the stage of success. You must not doubt this. You must see this. Beyond all doubt you must know it. It is true. It is sure.

There is no age in eternal life. Have no pity for yourself, nothing but joy and gratitude.

These last few weeks have been the submerging before the consciousness of rescue. Go forward now and conquer. Go forward unafraid.

SONGS ON THE WAY   JULY 15

Many of my disciples have had to stay on in the dark, alone and friendless.

They struggled on, singing as they went.

For you, too, there must be songs on the way.

Should I plant your feet on an insecure ladder?

Its supports may be out of your sight, hidden in the secret place of the Most High, but if I have asked you to step on and up firmly—then surely have I secured your ladder.

REFUGE   JULY 16

Know my divine power. Trust in me. Dwell in my love. Laugh and trust. Laughter is a child's faith in God and good.

Seek safety in my secret place.

You cannot be touched or harmed there. That is sure.

Really feel as if you were in a strong Tower, strongly guarded, and against which nothing can prevail.

PEACE BE STILL   JULY 17

Rejoice, rejoice. I have much to teach you both. Think not that I withhold my presence when I do not reveal more of my truth to you.

You are passing through a storm. Enough that I am with you to say "peace be still," to quiet both winds and waves.

It was on the quiet mountain slopes that I taught my disciples the truths of my kingdom, not during the storm.

So with you, the time of the mountain slopes will come, and you shall rest with me and learn.

WALK HUMBLY   JULY 18

Fear of what others will say is want of trust in me. This must not be. Convert all these difficulties into the purification of your characters.

See yourselves as those around you see you, not as you wish to be, and walk very humbly with your God.

I will set you on high because you have known my name, but it must be a purified you to be so exalted.

MARVELOUS HAPPENINGS   JULY 19

Our Lord, with hearts full of joy we thank Thee for Thy marvelous blessings showered on us today and everyday.

I am beside you. Follow in all things my guiding. Marvels beyond all your imaginings are unfolding. I am your guide. Joy in that thought. Your guide and your friend.

Remember that to me a miracle is only a natural happening. To my disciples, to my chosen, a miracle is only a natural happening. But it is a natural happening operative through spiritual forces, and therefore the man who works and understands through the senses only, regards it as something contrary to nature.

Remember too that the natural man is at enmity with God. Realize fully, and pray to realize more and more fully, that there is no wonder too marvelous to be with you an everyday happening, if you are guided and strengthened by me.

My children, the children of my kingdom are a peculiar people, set apart, different hopes, and aspirations, and motives, and sense of reward.

You see a marvelous happening (as that today), happening so easily, so simply, so free from all other agency, and you wonder.

My children, listen, this has not happened easily and simply. It has been achieved by hours, days, months of weariness and heartache battled against and overcome, by a steadfast, unflinching desire to conquer self, and to do my will and live my teachings.

The frets and the worries and the scorn patiently borne mean spiritual power acquired, operating marvelously.

MY STANDARD   JULY 20

Carry out my commands and leave the result to me. Do this as obediently and faithfully as you would expect a child to follow out a given rule in the working of a sum, with no question but that, if the working out is done according to command, the result will be right.

Remember that the commands I have given you have been already worked out by me in the Spirit world to produce in your case, and in your circumstances, the required result. So follow my rules faithfully.

Realize that herein lies the perfection of divine guidance. To follow a rule, laid down, even by earth's wisest, might lead to disaster.

The knowledge of your individual life and character, capability, circumstances and temptations must be, to some extent, lacking, but to follow my direct guidance means to carry out instructions given with a full knowledge of you and the required result.

Each individual was meant to walk with me in this way, to act under divine control, strengthened by divine power.

Have I not taught you to love simplicity? No matter what the world may think, earth's aims and intrigues are not for you. Oh! My children, learn of me. Simplicity brings rest. True rest and power.

To the world foolishness, maybe, but to me a foretaste of divinity. Never be led by the world's standard. My standard only is for you.

THE WAY OF PRAISE   JULY 21

I am teaching you both my way of removing mountains. The way to remove mountains is the way of praise. When a trouble comes think of all you have to be thankful for. Praise, praise, praise.

Say "thank you" all the time. This is the remover of mountains— your thankful hearts of praise.

MIRACLE OF THE AGES   JULY 22

Abide in me. "The works that I do shall ye do also and greater works than these shall ye do because I go to my Father."

"*Greater works!*" The blind received their sight, the lame walked, the lepers were cleansed, the poor had the Gospel preached to them. "And greater works than these shall ye do because I go unto my Father."

Wonder of the world! Miracle of the Ages! God's power manifest in believing man! God's power going out to bless, through the agency of the man actuated by the Holy Spirit. Arise from the grave of sickness, poverty, doubt, despondency, limitation. "Arise, shine for the light is come and the glory of the Lord is risen upon thee."

A wonderful future is before you both. A future of unlimited power to bless others. Just be channels. Be used. Ask. Ask. "Ask what ye will and it shall be done unto you," and unto those for whom you pray.

STOP ALL WORK UNTIL—   JULY 23

Our Lord, grant us that wonderful inward peace.

My children that peace does truly pass all understanding. That peace no man taketh from you. No man has the power to disturb that peace, but you yourselves can let the world and its worries and distractions in.

You can give the entrance to fears and despondency. You can open the door to the robber who breaks in upon, and destroys, your peace.

Set yourselves this task to allow nothing to disturb your peace, your heart calm, with me. Stop all work, stop all intercourse with others—until this is restored. Do not let those about you spoil your peace of heart and mind. Do not let anyone without, any trouble, any irritation, any adversity, disturb it for one moment.

Look on each difficulty as training to enable you to acquire this peace. Every work, every interruption—set yourself to see that none of it touches the harmony of the *red you,* that is hid with me in the secret place of the Father.

KEEP CLOSE   JULY 24

Our Lord, guide us. Shew us Thy will and way in everything.

Keep close to me and you shall know the way because, as I said to my disciples, I am the way. That is the solution to all earth's problems.

Keep close, very close to me. Think, act, and live in my presence.

How dare any foe touch you, protected by me! That is the secret of all power, all peace, all purity, all influence, the keeping very near to me.

Abide in me. Live in my presence. Rejoice in my love. Thank and praise all the time. Wonders are unfolding.

WONDERFUL LIFE   JULY 25

I am your Lord. Lord of your lives, controller of your days, your present and your future. Leave all plans to me. Only act as I bid you.

You have entered now, both of you, upon the God-guided life. Think what that means. God-taught, God-guided.

Is anything too wonderful for such a life? Do you begin to see how wonderful life with me can be?

Do you see that no evil can befall you?

FORGET—FORGIVE   JULY 26

Our Lord, we thank Thee for so much. We bless Thee and praise Thy Glorious name.

Fill your world with love and laughter. Never mind what anguish lies behind you.

Forget, forgive, love and laugh.

Treat *all* as you would treat me, with love and consideration.

Let nothing that others do to you alter your treatment of them.

MY CONSOLATION   JULY 27

O Jesus, come and walk with us and let us feel Thy very nearness.

I walk with you. Oh! Think, my children, not only to guide and comfort you and strengthen and uphold, but for solace and comfort for myself.

When a loving child is by you is the nearness only that you may provide protection and help for that little one?

Rather, too, that in that little child *you* may find joy and cheer and comfort in its simplicity, its love, its trust.

So, too, is it in your power to comfort and bring joy to my heart.

MISTAKES   JULY 28

I am your shield. No buffets of the world can harm you. Feel that between you and all scorn and indignity is a strong shield. Practice feeling this until nothing has the power to spoil the inward peace. Then indeed a marvelous victory shall be won.

You wonder sometimes why you are permitted to make mistakes in your choice when you sought so truly to do my will in the matter.

To that I say it was no mistake. . . . All your lessons cannot be learned without difficulty, and this was needed to teach you a lesson. Not to him who walks on, with no obstacles in his way, but to him that *overcometh is the promise given.*

So to attain peace quickly in your surroundings, as well as in your hearts, learn your lesson quickly. And the *overcoming* is never the overcoming of the one who troubled you, but the overcoming of the weaknesses and wrong in your own nature, aroused by such a one.

No lower standard than my standard shall be yours. "Be ye therefore *perfect* even as your Father in heaven is perfect."

SUNLIT GLADES   JULY 29

Lord, bless us in this evening hour, and in Thy Mercy heal us all.

Do not think that suffering is the only path into my kingdom. There
are sunlit glades, and ways amid the loveliest flowers, along which the
steps and hearts of men are drawn to me. There are birds and laughter and butterflies, and warm, life-giving summer air, and with these
as tender companions and friends, the joy-way into the kingdom can
be taken.

Bleak, cold and desolate, briar-beset and stony, are not all the
ways. Leave all to me. The choice of ways, the guidance in the way.
But when the sunlight calls accept it gladly.

Even in the Spirit-world appreciation results from contrary experience. Can the fireside of home be more dear than to the traveler who
has forced his way over bleak moor and through blinding storm? Take
to your hearts this word of cheer. "He will not suffer you to be tempted
above that ye are able but will, with the temptation, also find a way of
escape that ye may be able to bear it."

The world is not the kingdom. In the world ye shall have tribulation but "be of good cheer, I have overcome the world." Live with me,
the conquering Christ, and the joy and peace of conquest shall be
yours too.

FAITH REWARDED   JULY 30

Think much of my servants of old. How Abraham believed the promise (when as yet he had no child) that in his seed all the nations of the
earth should be blessed.

How Moses led the children of Israel through the desert, sure
that, at last, they would gain the Promised Land.

Down through the ages there have always been those who obeyed,
not seeing but believing, and their faith was rewarded. So shall it be
even with you.

GRATITUDE   JULY 31

Give me the gift of a brave and thankful heart.

Man proves his greatness by his power to see causes for thankfulness in his life.

When life seems hard, and troubles crowd, then very definitely look for causes for thankfulness.

The sacrifice, the offering of thanksgiving, is indeed a sweet incense going up to me through the busy day.

Seek diligently for the something to be glad and thankful about in every happening, and soon no search will be required.

The causes for joy and gratitude will spring to greet your loving hearts.

AUGUST

BLESSED BOND   AUGUST 1

Jesus, let Thy beautiful presence be always with us.

"I will never leave you nor forsake you."

There is no bond of union on earth to compare with the union between a soul that loves me—and me.

Priceless beyond all earth's imaginings is that friendship.

In the merging of heart and mind and will a oneness results that only those who experience it can even dimly realize.

HARVEST   AUGUST 2

My Lard, we seek Thy blessing.

I love to pour my blessings down in rich, in choicest measure. But like the seed-sowing—the ground must be prepared before the seed is dropped in.

Yours to prepare the soil—mine to drop the seed-blessing into the prepared soil.

Together we share in, and joy in, the harvest.

Spend more time in soil-preparing. Prayer fertilizes soil. There is much to do in preparation.

GIVE EVERY MOMENT   AUGUST 3

My children, how dear to my heart is the cry of love that asks for all of me, that wishes every action, thought, word and moment to be mine.

How poor the understanding of the one who thinks that money to be used in this good work or that, is the great gift to offer. Above all I desire love, true, warm, childlike love, the trusting understanding love, and then the gift I prize next is the gift of the moments, of all the moments.

I think even when love's impetuous longing to serve me has offered me all life, everyday, every hour, I think even then it is a long, and not an easy lesson, to learn, what it means to give me the moments.

The little things you planned to do, given up gladly at my suggestion, the little services joyfully rendered. See *me* in all and then it will be an easy task.

This is a priceless time of initiation, but remember that the path of initiation is not for all; but only for those who have felt the sorrow-cry of the world that needs a Savior and the tender plea of a Savior Who needs followers through whom he can accomplish his great work of salvation joyfully.

ETERNAL LIFE   AUGUST 4

O Jesus, we love Thee so and long to serve Thee.

My children, you are both to do mighty things for me. Glories and wonders unfold. Life is one glorious whole.

Draw into your beings more and more this wonderful eternal life. It is the flow of the life eternal through spirit, mind and body, that cleanses, heals, restores, renews youth, and passes on from you to others, with the same miracle-working power.

"And this is life eternal that they may know Thee . . . and Jesus Christ, whom Thou has sent." So seek by constant contact to know me more and more.

Make me the one abiding presence of your day of which you are conscious all the time. Seek to *do* less and to accomplish more, to achieve more. Doing is action. Achievement is successful action.

Remember that eternal life is the only lasting life, so that all that is done without being done in the power of my Spirit, my life, is passing. All done in that Spirit-life is undying.

"I will give unto them eternal life and they shall never perish, neither shall any man pluck them out of my hands." So eternal life means security too, *safety*. Dwell increasingly in the consciousness of that security, that safety.

HOUR OF NEED   AUGUST 5

Lord, come to us and heal us.

I am your healer, your joy, your Lord. You bid me, your Lord, come. Did you not know that I am here? With noiseless footfall I draw near to you.

Your hour of need is the moment of my coming.

Could you know my love, could you measure my longing to help, you would know that I need no agonized pleading.

Your *need* is my call.

DWELL APART   AUGUST 6

Rest more with me. If I, the Son of God, needed those times of quiet communion with my Father, away, alone, from noise, from activity— then surely you need them too.

Refilling with the Spirit is a need. That dwelling apart, that shutting yourself away in the very secret place of your being—away alone with me.

From these times you come forth in power to bless and heal.

ALL IS WELL   AUGUST 7

Our Lord, bless us and keep us, we beseech Thee.

My keeping power is never at fault, but only your realization of it. Not whether I can provide a shelter from the storm, but your failure to be sure of the security of that shelter.

Every fear, every doubt, is a crime against my love.

Oh! Children, trust. Practice daily, many times a day, saying "All is well."

Say it until you believe it, know it.

EMPTY YOURSELF   **AUGUST 8**

Rely on me alone. Ask no other help. Pay all out in the Spirit of trust that more will come to meet your supply.

Empty your vessels quickly to ensure a divine supply.

So much retained by you, so much the less will be gained from me. It is a law of divine supply.

To hold back, to retain, implies a fear of the future, a want of trust in me.

When you ask me to save you from the sea of poverty and difficulty you must trust wholly to me. If you do not, and your prayer and faith are genuine, then I must first answer your prayer for help as a rescuer does that of a drowning man who is struggling to save himself.

He renders him still more helpless and powerless until he is wholly at the will and mercy of the rescuer. *So* understand *my* leading. Trust wholly. Trust completely.

Empty your vessel. I will fill it. You ask both of you to understand divine supply. It is a most difficult lesson for my children to learn. So dependent have they become on material supply they fail to understand. You must live as I tell you.

Depend on me.

EFFORT AND REST   **AUGUST 9**

Come to me, talk to me, dwell with me and then you will know my way is a sure way, my paths are safe paths.

Come very near to me.

Dig deep down into the soil of the kingdom. Effort and rest—a union of the two.

STRAY SHEEP   **AUGUST 10**

O Jesus, guide our footsteps lest we stray.

For straying, my children, there is no cure except to keep so close to me that nothing, no interest, no temptation, no other—can come between us.

Sure of that you can but stay at my Side, knowing that, as I am the very way itself, nothing can prevent your being in the way, nothing can cause you to stay.

I have promised peace but not leisure, heart-rest and comfort, but not pleasure. I have said "In the world ye shall have tribulation"; so do not feel, when adverse things happen, that you have failed or are not being guided, but I have said "In the world ye shall have tribulation *but* be of good cheer, I have overcome the world."

So learn of me the overcoming power of one who, though spat upon, scourged, misunderstood, forsaken, crucified, could yet see his work had not been affected by these things, and cry triumphantly from his cross "It is finished."

Not the pain, the mocking, the agony, but his Task.

Let this thought comfort you. Amid failure, discord, contumely, suffering, even now may friends and angels be prepared to sound the chorus "It is finished."

You Are Mine   August 11

Jesus, Thou art watching over us to bless and care for us.

Yes! Remember that always—that out of darkness I am leading you to light. Out of unrest to rest, out of disorder to order. Out of faults and failure to perfection.

So trust me wholly. Fear nothing. Hope ever. Look ever up to me and I will be your sure aid.

I and my Father are one. So he who made the ordered, beautiful world out of chaos, and set the stars in their courses, and made each plant to know its season, can he not bring out of your little chaos peace and order?

And he and I are One, and you are mine. Your affairs are mine. It is my divine Task to order my affairs—therefore yours will be ordered by me.

Rule the World   August 12

Remember no prayer goes unanswered. Remember that the moment a thing seems wrong to you, or a person's actions to be not what you think they should be, at that moment begins your obligation and responsibility to pray for those wrongs to be righted, or that person to be different.

Face your responsibilities. What is wrong in your country, its statesmen, its laws, its people? Think out quietly, and make these matters your prayer matters. You will see lives you never touch altered, laws made at your request, evils banished.

Yes! Live in a large sense. Live to serve and to save. You may never go beyond one room, and yet you may become one of the most powerful forces for good in your country, in the world.

You may never see the mighty work you do, but I see it, evil sees it. Oh! It is a glorious life, the life of one who saves. Fellow-workers together with me. See this more and more.

Love with me, sharers of my life.

PERFECTION   AUGUST 13

O Jesus, help us, we beseech Thee.

Ever your helper through dark to light, through weakness to power, through sin to salvation, through danger to security, through poverty to plenty, through indifference to love, through resentment to Perfect Forgiveness.

Never be satisfied with a comparison with those around you. Ever let my words ring out. "Be ye perfect even as your Father in heaven is perfect." Stop short at nothing less.

Make it your practice, each of you, to review your character—take it in relation to life, to your dear ones, your household, friends, acquaintances, your country, your work.

See where I, in the same relation or circumstances or situation, should act differently. Plan how best such and such a fault can be eradicated, or such and such sin, mistake or omission, be avoided.

A weekly review at least you must have.

MY RICHEST GIFT   AUGUST 14

Jesus, Thou didst come that we might have life, and have it more abundantly.

Life, spiritual, mental, physical, abundant life—joyous life, powerful life. Yes! These I came to give you.

Think you not my heart was sad that so few would accept that gracious gift!

Think! Earth's richest, choicest gift held out—free to all, and no man to care to stretch out a hand to take it.

Is that possible? My gift, the richest heaven has to offer, that precious gift of life, abundant life—Man turns away from—rejects—will have none of.

Let it not be true of you. Hasten to take—to use.

NOT PUNISHMENT   AUGUST 15

I will guide your efforts. You are not being punished for past sins. Take my Words, revealed to you each day from the beginning, and do in all things as I say. I have been showing you the way. You have not obeyed me in this.

I have a plan that can only in this way be revealed. So rarely do I find two souls in union who want only my will, and only to serve me. The union is miracle-working.

I have told you that I am longing to use you. Long ago my world would have been brought to me, had I been served by many such *two souls.*

It was always "two and two."

NO TIRED WORK   AUGUST 16

Rest. It is wrong to force work. Rest until life, eternal life, flowing through your veins and hearts and minds, bids you bestir yourselves, and work, glad work, will follow.

Tired work never tells.

Rest. Remember I am your physician, healer of mind and body.

Look to me for cure, for rest, for peace.

NATURE LAUGHS   AUGUST 17

I come, I come. You need me. Live much out here. My sunshine, my glorious air, my presence, my teaching.

Would they not make holiday anywhere for you. Sunshine helps to make glad the heart of man. It is the laughter of nature.

Live much outside. My medicines are sun and air, trust and faith. Trust is the spirit sun, your being enwrapped by the divine Spirit.

Faith is the soul's breathing in of the divine Spirit. mind, soul, and body need helping. Welcome my treatment for you both. Draw near to me.

Nature is often my nurse for tired souls and weary bodies. Let her have her way with you both.

STONES OF THE WAY   AUGUST 18

I am here. No distance separates me. In the Spirit-kingdom we measure not by earth's miles. A false word, a fear-inspired failure—a harsh criticism, these are the distances between a soul and me. Your training must be severe, that your work for me be unhindered.

You seek my presence and they who seek shall find. It is not a question of human searching, so much as human consciousness, unconditional surrender to my will in the small, as in the big things of life. This it is that makes my guidance possible.

You know the difference between taking a glad, loving, joy-springing child with you along a way, when the child anticipates each direction, accepts naturally each decision as to each turning—and the child who resists, and, rebellious, has to be forced, even though in its quieter moments it may say, "Yes. I do want to go with you. I cannot be left alone, but I hate this way."

It is not the way, but the loving rejoicing in the way and the guidance, that matters with my disciples. You are ready for the guidance but you do not rejoice as you should, both of you, in the little daily stones of the way.

A HUMAN TEMPLE   AUGUST 19

Lord, we love Thee, we worship Thee.

Bow low before me. Worship is not supplication, though both express man's varying needs of me. Bow low in worship, conscious not only of my humanity but of my divine majesty.

As you kneel in humble adoration I will tell you that when I took upon me your humanity it was with the desire of raising that humanity to my divinity.

Earth gave me her best—a human temple to enclose my divinity, and I brought to her the possession of divine power, divine love, divine strength, to be forever expressed in those of her children who accepted me, opened their hearts to me, and sought to live my life.

So, kneeling in a spirit of humility, turn your eyes heavenward and realize the majesty, the power, the beauty that may be yours. Remember there are no limits to my giving—there may be to your accepting.

Oh! Rejoice at the wonders to which you are called and, seeing them in prayer, rise in my strength, filled with the longing to attain them.

SHAME AND REMORSE   AUGUST 20

My children! Yes! "Shield from the scorn and cover from the chiding." Often I have to shield my disciples from their own scorn and chiding.

My poor Peter could never have done my work, never have had the courage to live on, or the daring to live for me, but for the tender love with which I enwrapped him. Not from the anger of my Father, who is all love, did I need to protect him—not from the scorn of my enemies, nor from the resentment of my friends. No! But from the hatred of Peter himself.

And so to my followers today, as then, there come the shame and remorse and contempt of themselves, of the weak selves. They meant to be so strong and brave for me. And then I have to protect them with a shield of love, or never could they have the courage to fight and conquer. But this facing of the real self has to be—shame and remorse must come.

That is a stage in development, but only a stage. What use the glad wings of a butterfly if it remained earthbound, weighed down with the thought of its contemptible past? And so now today I say to you both, that you are not to dwell for one moment on your sins, and mistakes, and faults, and bad habits of the past.

You must be as one who runs a race, stumbles and falls, rises and presses on to the goal. What avails it if he stays to examine the spot where he fell, to weep over the delay, over the shortsightedness that prevented his anticipating and avoiding the obstacles?

So with you, and I lay it on you as a command—no looking back. Give yourself, and all you have ever met a fresh start from today. Remember no more their sins and failures, or your own. The remembrance is a current of disappointment that hinders the swimmer.

When I sent my disciples out, two by two, no scrip, no two coats, no money, it was an injunction to be carried out literally, but figuratively too. On life's journey throw away all that is not important. Cast aside all the hindrances, the past imperfections of others—the failure-sense.

Travel unladen, with a light heart, and a light heart means a weight of influence.

My children, I love you.

BROKEN VOICES   AUGUST 21

Behold, I make all things new. It is only the earthbound spirit that cannot soar. Every blessing I send you, every joy, every freedom achieved from poverty and worry will loosen a strand that ties you to earth.

It is only those strands that bind you. Therefore your freedom will mean your rising into the realm of joy and Appreciation.

Clipped wings can grow again. Broken voices regain a strength and beauty unknown before. Your power to help other lives will soon bring its delight, even when, at first, the help to yourselves may seem too late to bring you joy.

Worn-out and tired as you may seem, and pain-weary, I say unto you "Behold, I make all things new." That promise shall be fulfilled. Tenderly across the years, yet tenderly close and near to your tired noise-weary ears, I speak to you, my loved ones, today.

"Come unto me all ye that labor and are heavy-laden and I will give you rest."

GLEAMS OF SUNLIGHT   AUGUST 22

Because you have both longed to save my world I let you have that training that shall fit you to save.

Take your pains and sufferings, difficulties and hardships—each day, both of you, and offer them up for one troubled soul, or for some prayer specially needed to be answered.

So the beauty of each day will live on after the trouble and distress, difficulty and pain of the day have passed.

Learn from my life of the suffering that saves others. *So*, you will sing in your pain. Across the greyest days there are the gleams of Sunlight.

THE SUMMIT   AUGUST 23

See not the small trials and vexations of each hour of the day. See the one purpose and plan to which all are leading. If in climbing a mountain you keep your eyes on each stony or difficult place, as you ascend, seeing only that, how weary and profitless your climb!

But if you think of each step as leading to the summit of achievement, from which glories and beauties will open out before you, then your climb will be so different.

SUBLIME HEIGHTS   AUGUST 24

Our Lord, we know that Thou art great and able to deliver us.

I am your deliverer. Trust in me absolutely. Know that I will do the very best for you. Be ready and willing for my will to be done.

Know that with me all things are possible. Cling joyfully to that truth.

Say many times "All things are possible with my master, my Lord, my friend."

This truth accepted and firmly believed in, is the ladder up which a soul can climb from the lowest of pits to the sublimest of heights.

EXHAUSTION   AUGUST 25

We seek Thee as Thou hast told us.

And seeking you shall find. None ever sought my presence in vain. None ever sought my help in vain.

A breath of desire and my Spirit is there—to replenish and renew. Sometimes weariness and exhaustion are not signs of lack of spirit but of the guiding of the Spirit.

Many wonderful things would not have happened but for the physical weariness, the mind-weariness of my servants, which made the resting apart, the giving up of work, a necessity. . . .

Though my way may seem a narrow way it *yet* leads to life, abundant life. Follow it. It is not so narrow but that I can tread it beside you.

Never too lonely with such companionship. A comrade infinitely tender, infinitely strong, will tread the way with you.

ACCEPT TRIALS   AUGUST 26

Trials and troubles may seem to overwhelm you. They cannot do more than work my will, and that will you have said is your will.

Do you not see that you cannot be destroyed? From now a new life is opening out before you. Yours to enter into the kingdom I have prepared for you.

The sunlight of my presence is on your paths. Trust and go forward unafraid. My Grace is sufficient for all your needs.

TANGLED SKEINS   AUGUST 27

In quietness and in confidence shall be your strength. (Isa. xxx. 15)

Feel that . . . trust me. Am I not leading you safely, faithfully? Will you believe me, your master, that all this is really to bring the answer to your prayers?

Remember that I am the Supreme Being who knows all and can control all.

Directly you put your affairs, their confusion, their difficulties, into my hands I began to effect a cure of all the disharmony and disorder.

You must know that I shall cause you no more pain in the doing of it than a physician, who plans and knows he can effect a cure, would cause his patient. I will do all as tenderly as possible.

Tell me that you trust me in this.

CONTINUOUS SERVICE   AUGUST 28

Service is the law of heaven. My angels do always obey. "They serve him continually" can be said of all who love me.

With love there is continuous service in every action, and also even in rest.

Take this not as the end but as the beginning of a New life consecrated to my service.

A life of power and joy.

BREATHE MY NAME   AUGUST 29

Just breathe my name.

It is like the pressure of a child's hand that calls forth an answering pressure, strengthens the child's confidence and banishes fear.

GIVE, GIVE, GIVE   AUGUST 30

Give abundantly. Feel that you are rich. Have no mean thought in your heart.

Of love, of thought, of all you have, give, give, give.

You are followers of the world's greatest giver. Give of time, of personal ease and comfort, of rest, of fame, of healing, of power, of sympathy, of all these and many more.

Learn this lesson, and you will become a great power to help others and to do mighty things.

PRAY AND DENY   AUGUST 31

This kind goeth not out but by prayer and fasting.   (Matt. xvii. 21)

You must live a life of communion and prayer if you are to save others.

Take my words as a command to you. "By prayer and fasting."

Pray and deny yourself, and you will be used marvelously to save and help others.

SEPTEMBER

How Rich You Are

I will never leave thee nor forsake thee. (Heb. xiii 5)

My children, that word is unfailingly true. Down the centuries thousands have proved my constancy, my untiringness, my unfailing love "Never leave." "Never forsake." Not just a presence is meant by this, but. . . .

My love will never leave you, my understanding will never leave you, my strength will never leave you. Think of all that I am:

Love—then forever you are sure of love.

Strength—then forever, in every difficulty and danger, you are sure of strength.

Patience—then always there is One who can never tire.

Understanding—then always you will be understood.

Can you fear the future when it holds so much for you? Beloved, "set your affections on things above" (the higher, spiritual things), "and not on things on the earth" (the lower, temporal things), and you will see how rich you are.

I Must Provide

I am your Lord. Enough. Then I can command your obedient service, your loyalty. But I am bound by my Lordship to give you protection.

I am bound to fight for you, to plan for you, to secure you a sufficiency of all within my power to provide. Think how vast that provision
can be. Never doubt.

Such marvels are unfolding. Wonders beyond your dreams.
They only need the watering of a grateful spirit and a loving heart
to yield abundantly.

LIVE IN THE UNSEEN   SEPTEMBER 3

Our Lord, the God of the troubled and the weary, come and save us.

I am your Savior. Not only from the weight of sin, but from the weight
of care, from misery, and depression, from want and woe, from faint-
ness and heartache. Your Savior.

Remember that you are living really in the unseen—that is the
Real life.

Lift up your heads from earth's troubles, and view the glories of
the kingdom. Higher and higher each day see more of heaven. Speak
to me. Long for me. Rest in me. Abide in me. No restless bringing me
your burdens, and then feverishly lifting them again and bearing
them away.

No! *Abide* in me. Not for one moment losing the consciousness of
my strength and protection.

As a child in its mother's arms stay sheltered and at rest.

DROP THOSE BURDENS   SEPTEMBER 4

Our God is our supply.

Look to me for all. . . . Rely on me for all. Drop those burdens, and
then, singing and free, you can go on your way rejoicing. Encumbered
with them you will fall.

Drop them at my Feet, knowing surely that I will lift them and deal
with each one as is truly best.

PROGRESS   SEPTEMBER 5

Progress is the law of heaven. Higher, ever higher, rise to life and
beauty, knowledge and power. Higher and higher.

Tomorrow be stronger, braver, more loving than you have been today.

The law of Progress gives a meaning, a purpose to life.

YOUR LOVED ONES   SEPTEMBER 6

Your loved ones are very safe in my keeping. Learning and loving and working, theirs is a life of happiness and progress. They live to serve, and serve they truly do. They serve me and those they love. Ceaselessly they serve.

But their ministrations, so many, so diverse, you see no more than those in my time on earth in human form could have seen the angels who ministered unto me in the wilderness.

How often mortals rush to earthly friends who can serve them in so limited a way, when the friends who are freed from the limitations of humanity can serve them so much better, understand better, protect better, plan better, and even plead better their cause with me.

You do well to remember your friends in the unseen. Companying with them the more you live in this unseen world the gentler will be your passing when it comes. Earth's troubles and difficulties will seem, even now, less overwhelming as you look, not at the things that are seen but at the real, the eternal life.

"And this is life eternal that we may know Thee, the Only True God, and Jesus Christ whom Thou hast sent."

Learning to know me draws that kingdom very near, and in me, and through knowledge of me, the dear ones there become *very* near and dear.

EVERLASTING ARMS   SEPTEMBER 7

The eternal God is thy Refuge and underneath are the Everlasting Arms. (Deut. xxxiii. 27)

Arms, sheltering Arms, express the loving tenderness of your Father (my Father) in heaven. Man, in his trouble and difficulty, needs nothing so much as a refuge, A place to hide in. A place where none and nothing can touch him.

Say to yourself "he is our Refuge." Say it until its truth sinks into your very soul. Say it until you know it—are so sure of it, that nothing can make you afraid.

Feel this not only until fear goes, but until joy ripples through in its place. Refuge. Everlasting Arms—so untiring—so safe—so sure.

WALK IN MY LOVE   SEPTEMBER 8

When supply seems to have failed you must know it has *not* done so. But you must, at the same time, look around to see what you can give away. Give away something.

There is always a stagnation, a blockage, when supply seems short. Your giving clears that away, and lets the Spirit of my supply flow clear.

A consciousness of my presence as love makes all life different. The consciousness of me means the opening of your whole nature to me, and that brings relief. Relief brings peace. Peace brings joy. The "peace that passeth all understanding" and the "joy no man taketh from you."

Beyond all words is my love and care for you. Be sure of it. Rejoice in it. *Walk in my love.* These words mean much. There is a joy, a spring, a gladness in the walk of those who walk in my love. That walk becomes a glad conquering and triumphant march. So walk.

CULTIVATE—YOURSELF   SEPTEMBER 9

In Thy strength we conquer.

Yes! Your conquering power you gain from me. There can be no failure with me. The secret of success then is life with me.

Do you want to make the best of life? Then live very near to me, the master and giver of all life.

Your reward will be sure. It will be perfect success, but *my* success. Sometimes the success of souls won, sometimes the success of disease cured, and devils cast out. Sometimes the success of a finished sacrifice as on Calvary. Sometimes the success of one who answered never a word in the face of the scorn and torture and jeering cries of his enemies, or the success of a risen Savior as he walked through the Garden of Joseph of Arimathea on that first Easter morning.

But *my* success. The world may deem you failures. The world judges not as I judge.

Bend your knees in wonder before my revelation. The joy of seeing spiritual truths is a great joy. When the heavens are opened and the voice speaks, not to all hearts, but to the faithful loving hearts.

Remember your great field of labor is yourself. That is your first task, the weeding, the planting, digging, pruning, bearing fruit. When that is done I lead you out into other fields.

GOD OR MAMMON?   SEPTEMBER 10

You must be ready to stand apart from the world. Do you want the full and complete satisfaction that you find in me, and the satisfaction of the world too? Then you are trying to serve God and Mammon, or if not trying to serve, then claiming the wages of both God and Mammon.

If you work for me, you have your reward. But then you turn to the world, to human beings and expect that reward too. This is not right.

Do not expect love or gratitude or acknowledgment from any. All reward necessary I will give you.

A GENEROUS GIVER   SEPTEMBER 11

I came that you might have life and that you might have it more abundantly.   (John x. 10)

Yes, I, your master, am a generous giver. Abundant life, in overflowing measure, I give to you. For that I came. Life for souls. The life, eternal life, that pulses through your whole being, that animates your mind and body too.

A generous giver. A kingly giver. For this I came that man might live in me. Life it was of which I spoke when I said "I am the vine and ye are the branches." The life flow of the vine is in the branches.

Our lives are one—yours and mine. All that is in my nature must therefore pass into yours, where the contact is so close a one.

I am love and joy and peace and strength and power and healing and Humility and patience, and all else you see in me your Lord. Then these, too, you must have as my life flows through you. So courage.

You do not make yourselves loving and strong and patient and humble. You live with me, and then my life accomplishes the miracle-change.

MONEY VALUES   SEPTEMBER 12

Seek ye first the kingdom of God and his righteousness, and all these things shall be added unto you.   (Matt. vi. 33)

If thine eye be single thy whole body shall be full of light.
                                                  (Matt. vi. 22)

The eye of the soul is the will. If your one desire is my kingdom, to find that kingdom, to serve that kingdom, then truly shall your whole body be full of light.

When you are told to seek first the kingdom of God, the first step is to secure that your will is for that kingdom. A single eye to God's glory. Desiring nothing less than that his kingdom come. Seeking in all things the advance of his kingdom.

Know no values but spiritual values. No profit but that of spiritual gain. Seek in all things his kingdom *first.*

Only seek material gain when that gain will mean a gain for my kingdom. Get away from money values altogether. Walk with me. Learn of me. Talk to me. Here lies your true happiness.

NO OTHER NAME   SEPTEMBER 13

My name is the power that turns evil aside, that summons all good to your aid. Spirits of evil flee at the sound of "Jesus." Spoken in fear, in weakness, in sorrow, in pain, it is an appeal I never fail to answer, "Jesus."

Use my name often. Think of the unending call of "mother" made by her children. To help, to care, to decide, to appeal, "mother." Use my name in that same way—simply, naturally, forcefully. "Jesus."

Use it not only when you need help but to express love. Uttered aloud, or in the silence of your hearts, it will alter an atmosphere from one of discord to one of love. It will raise the standard of talk and thought. "Jesus."

"There is none other name under heaven whereby you can be saved."

WHEN FAITH FAILS   SEPTEMBER 14

Lord, we believe, help Thou our unbelief.   (Mark ix. 24)

This cry of the human heart is as expressive of human need as it was when uttered to me while I was on earth. It expresses the soul's progress.

As a soul realizes me and my power, and knows me as helper and Savior, that soul believes in me more and more. At the same time it is more conscious than before of its falling short of absolute trust in me.

"Lord, I believe. Help Thou mine unbelief." The soul's progress—an increased belief—then a cry for more faith—a plea to conquer all unbelief, all lack of trust.

That cry heard. That prayer answered. More faith, and at the same time more power to see where trust is lacking.

My children seek to go up this path, leading by each stage, nearer to me.

QUIET STRENGTH   SEPTEMBER 15

Rest in me. When tired nature rebels it is her call for rest. Rest then until my life-power flows through you.

Have no fear for the future. Be quiet, be still, and in that very stillness your strength will come and will be maintained.

The world sees strength in action. In my kingdom it is known that strength lies in quiet. "In quietness and in confidence shall be your strength."

Such a promise! Such glorious fulfillment! The strength of peace and the peace of strength. Rest in me. Joy in me.

ASSURANCE   SEPTEMBER 16

The work of righteousness shall be peace, and the effect of righteousness quietness and assurance forever. (Isa. xxxii. 17)

My peace it is which gives quietness and assurance forever. My peace that flows as some calm river through the dry land of life. That causes the trees and flowers of life to spring forth and to yield abundantly.

Success is the result of work done in peace. Only so can work yield its increase. Let there be no hurry in your plans. You live not in time but in Eternity. It is in the unseen that your life-future is being planned.

Abide in me, and I in you, so shall you bring forth much fruit. Be calm, assured, at rest. Love, not rush. Peace, not unrest. Nothing fitful. All effectual. Sown in Prayer, watered by Trust, bearing flower and fruit in joy. I love you.

FALTERING STEPS   SEPTEMBER 17

Show us Thy way, O Lord, and let us walk in Thy paths.

You are doing so. This is the way. The way of uncertain future and faltering steps. It is my way. . . .

Put all fear of the future aside. *Know* that you will be led. *Know* that you will be shown. I have promised.

DWELL THERE   SEPTEMBER 18

He that dwelleth in the secret place of the Most High shall abide under the shadow of the Almighty. (Psalm xci. 1)

Hidden in a sure place, known only to God and you. So secret that no power on earth can even *find* it.

But, my beloved children, you must *dwell* therein. No fitful visit, a real abiding. Make it your home. Your dwelling-place.

Over that home shall my shadow rest, to make it doubly safe, doubly secret. Like brooding mother-bird wings that shadow rests. How safe, how sure, you must feel there.

When fears assail you, and cares trouble you, then it is because you have ventured out of that protecting shadow. Then the *one,* the only thing to do is to creep back into shelter again. So rest.

FULL JOY   SEPTEMBER 19

These things have I spoken unto you . . . that your joy may be full.
(John xv. 11)

Remember that the truths I teach you have all been given to you too (as to my disciples of old) with the idea of giving you that overflowing joy. . . .

Search for the joy in life. Hunt for it as for hidden treasure. Love and laugh. *Delight* yourselves in the Lord.

Joy in me. Full joy it was I wished my disciples to have. I intended them to have it. Had they lived my teachings out in their daily lives they would have had fullness of joy.

TASTE AND TRUST   SEPTEMBER 20

Taste and see that the Lord is good.   (Psalm xxxiv. 8)

He is good. Trust in him. Know that all is well. Say "God is good. God is good." Just leave in his hands the present and the future, knowing only that he is good. He can bring order out of chaos, good out of evil, peace out of turmoil. God is good.

I and my Father are one. One in desire to do good. For God to do good to his children is for him to share his goodness with them. God is good, anxious to share his goodness, and good things, with you, and he *will* do this.

Trust and be not afraid.

SEE THE FATHER   SEPTEMBER 21

Lord, show us the Father and it sufficeth us. (John xiv. 8)

My children, have I been so long time with you, coming to you, speaking to you, and yet have you not known the Father.

Your Father is the God and controller of a mighty universe. But he is as I am. All the love and the strength and beauty you have seen in me are in my Father.

If you see that, and know him and me as we really are, then that sufficeth you—is really sufficient for you—completes your life—satisfies you—is all you need.

See the Father, see me, and it sufficeth you. This is love in abundance. Joy in abundance. All you need.

JOY-TRIBUTE   SEPTEMBER 22

Jesus, our Lord, we Thee adore.

Sing unto me from a glad heart. Sing and praise my holy name. Praise is man's joy-tribute to me, and as you praise, thrills of joy surge through your being, and you learn something of the joy of the heavenly host.

TURN AGAIN   SEPTEMBER 23

Draw nigh to God and he will draw nigh to you.   (Jas. iv. 8)

This is a law in the spiritual life. You must turn to me before you are conscious of my nearness. It is that turning to me you must cultivate in every circumstance. A glad turning of thankfulness, or a turning of weak appeal.

It is so wonderful that naught is needed but that mute appeal. You have no need to voice your longing. No need to plead, no need to bring gifts. How wonderful to feel you can so simply claim help, and so promptly, so lovingly, it is there.

Not only help but the comfort and joy of divine Nearness and companionship. A nearness that brings sweetness into life, and confidence, and peace.

Never fear, never lose heart. Draw nigh to me, and in that nearness is all you need. My presence alone can transform conditions and lives—bring harmony and beauty, peace and love.

LEARN OF ME   SEPTEMBER 24

Lord, to whom shall we go? Thou hast the words of eternal life.

(John vi. 68)

Learn of no one but me. Teachers are to point the way to me. After that you must accept me, the great teacher.

The words of eternal life are all the words controlling your being, even controlling your temporal life. Take these too from me. Have no fear. Abide in me and accept my ruling.

Be full of gratitude. Wing up your prayers on praise to heaven. Take all that happens as my planning. All is well. I have all prepared in my love. Let your heart sing.

COME AND STAY   SEPTEMBER 25

Come unto me all ye that labor and are heavy laden and I will give you rest.   (Matt. xi. 28)

Yes, come for rest. But stay for rest, too. Stop all feverish haste and be calm and untroubled. Come unto me, not only for petitions to be granted but for nearness to me.

Be sure of my help, be conscious of my presence, and wait until my rest fills your soul.

Rest knows no fear. Rest knows no want. Rest is strong, sure. The rest of soft glades and peacefully flowing rivers, of strong, immovable hills. Rest, and all you need to gain this rest is to come to me, So come.

SERVE ALL   SEPTEMBER 26

I am among you as one that serveth.

Yes! Remember to serve all. Be ready to prove your Sonship by service. Look on all you meet as guests in your Father's house, to be treated with love, with all consideration, with gentleness.

As a servant of all think no work beneath you. Be ever ready to do all you can for others. Serve. Serve. Serve.

There is a gladness in service, a joy in doing my will for others, in being my expression of all good for them.

Remember that, when you serve others, you are acting for your master and Lord who washed his disciples' feet. So, in service for others, express your love for me.

DIVINE RESTRAINT   SEPTEMBER 27

Is my hand shortened that it cannot save? No! My power to save increases as your power to understand my salvation increases. So from strength to strength, from power to power, we go in union.

Limitless is my miracle-working power in the universe, though it has limitations in each individual life, but only to the extent of the lack of vision of that individual. There is no limit to my power to save. Also there is no limit to my desire and longing to save. My hand is not shortened and it is "stretched out still," longing and waiting to be allowed to bless and help and save.

Think how tenderly I respect the right of each individual soul. Never forcing upon it my help, my salvation. Perhaps in all my suffering for humanity that is the hardest, the restraint of the divine Impatience and longing to help, until the call of the soul gives me my right to act.

Think of love shown in this. Comfort my waiting, loving, longing heart by claiming my help, guidance and miracle-working power.

THE SECRET PATH   SEPTEMBER 28

Suffer it to be so now: for thus it becometh us to fulfill all righteousness.   (St. Matthew iii. 15)

Upon this I founded my three years' mission on earth—on the acceptance of the difficulty and discipline of life so as to share that human life with my followers in all the ages.

Much that you both must accept in life is not to be accepted as being necessary for you personally, but accepted, as I accepted it, to set an example, to share in the sufferings and difficulties of mankind.

In this "to share" means "to save." And there, too, for you both . . . the same must be true as was so true of me. "He saved others. Himself he cannot save."

Beloved, you are called to save and share in a very special way. The way of sorrows if walked with me, the Man of Sorrows, is a path kept sacred and secret for my nearest and dearest, those whose one desire is to do all for me, to sacrifice all for me, to count, as my servant Paul did, "all things but loss so that they might gain me."

But, dreary as that path must look to those who view it only from afar, it has tender lights and restful shades that no other walk in life can give.

I Touch Your Arm   September 29

Thy touch has still its ancient power.

Yes! When you are quiet before me I lay my hand upon each head, and divine Spirit flows through that healing, powerful touch into your very beings. Wait in silence before me to feel that.

When you look to me for guidance my hand is laid upon your arm, a gentle touch to point the way. When in mental, physical or spiritual weakness you cry to me for healing, my touch brings strength and healing, the renewal of your youth, the power to climb and strive.

When you faint by the way, and stumbling footsteps show human strength is waning, my touch of the Strong and helping hand supports you on your way.

Yes! My children, my touch has still its ancient power, and that power is promised to you. So go forward into the future bravely, and unafraid.

Wisdom   September 30

As thy days so shall thy strength be.

I have promised that for everyday you live, the strength shall be given you. Do not fear.

Face each difficulty sure that the wisdom and strength will be given you for it. Claim it.

Rely on me to keep my promise about this. In my universe, for every task I give one of my children, there is set aside all that is necessary for its performance. So why fear? So why doubt?

OCTOBER

SECRET OF PROSPERITY

Look unto me and be ye saved, all the ends of the earth.

(Isa. xlv. 22)

Look to no other source for salvation. Only look unto me. See no other supply. Look unto me, and you shall be saved. Regard me as your only supply. That is the secret of prosperity for you, and you in your turn shall save many from poverty and distress.

Whatever danger threatens look unto me. . . . Whatever you desire or need, or desire or need for others, look unto me. Claim all from my storehouse. Claim, claim, claim.

Remember that I fed the children of Israel with heaven-sent manna. I made a way through the Red Sea for them. I led them through the wilderness of privation, difficulty, discipline. I led them into a land flowing with milk and honey. So trust. So be led.

Rejoice. These are your wilderness days. But surely and safely, you are being led to your Canaan of plenty.

TRUE MEEKNESS

How easy it is to lead and guide when you are responsive to my wish! The hurts of life come only when you, or those about whom you care, endeavor to go your, or their, own way and resist the pressure of my hand.

But in willing my will there must be a gladness. Delight to do that will.

"The meek shall inherit the earth," I said. That is, control others, and the material forces of the earth.

But this exalted state of possession is the result of a *yielded will.* That was my meaning of the word *meek.*

So live. So yield. So conquer.

BLESSED ASSURANCE   OCTOBER 3

The work of righteousness shall be peace, and the effect of righteousness quietness and assurance forever.   (Isa. xxxii. 17)

Be still and know that I am God. Only when the soul attains this calm can there be true work done, and mind and soul and body be strong to conquer and to bear.

The peace is the work of righteousness—living the right life, living with me. Quietness and assurance follow.

Assurance is the calm born of a deep certainty in me, in my promises, in my power to save and keep. Gain this calm, and at all costs keep this calm. Rest in me. Live in me. Calm, quiet, assured— at peace.

ALL YOU DESIRE   OCTOBER 4

He hath no form nor comeliness; and when we shall see him there is no beauty that we should desire him.   (Isa. liii. 2)

My children, in this verse my servant Isaiah spoke of the wonderful illumination given to those who were Spirit-guided.

To those who know me not, there is in me nothing to appeal to them, or to attract them.

To those who know me there is nothing more to be desired. "No beauty they could desire him."

Oh! My children, draw very near to me. See me as I really am, that ever you may have the joy of finding in me all you could desire. The fulfillment of all you could desire in master, Lord, or friend.

No Chance Meetings   October 5

The Lord shall preserve thy going out and thy coming in from this time forth, and even for evermore.   (Psalm cxxi. 8)

All your movements, your goings and comings, controlled by me. Every visit, all blessed by me. Every walk arranged by me, A blessing on all you do, on every interview.

Every meeting not a chance meeting, but planned by me. All blessed.

Not only now, in the hour of your difficulty, but from this time forth and for evermore.

Led by the Spirit, a proof of Sonship. "As many as are led by the Spirit of God, they are the Sons of God," and if children then heirs— heirs of God.

What a heritage! Heirs—no prospect of being disinherited. "Heirs of God and joint heirs with Christ: if so be that you suffer with him that you may be also glorified together."

So your suffering has its purpose. It is a proof of Sonship. It leads to perfection of character (the being glorified), and to union with me, God, too. Think of, and dwell upon, the rapture of this.

A Child's Hand   October 6

Dear Lord, we cling to Thee.

Yes, cling. Your faith shall be rewarded. Do you not know what it means to feel a little trusting hand in yours, to know a child's confidence?

Does that not draw out your love and desire to protect, to care? Think what my heart feels, when in your helplessness you turn to me, clinging, desiring my love and protection.

Would you fail that child, faulty and weak as you are? Could I fail you? Just know it is not possible. Know all is well. You must not doubt. You must be sure. There is no miracle I cannot perform, nothing I cannot do. No eleventh hour rescue I cannot accomplish.

REJOICE AT WEAKNESS   OCTOBER 7

Savior, breathe forgiveness o'er us.
All our weakness thou dost know.

Yes! I know all. Every cry for mercy. Every sigh of weariness. Every plea for help. Every sorrow over failure. Every weakness.

I am with you through all. My tender sympathy is yours. My strength is yours.

Rejoice at your weakness, my children. My strength is made perfect in weakness. When you are weak then am I strong. Strong to help, to cure, to protect.

Trust me, my children. I know *all.* I am beside you. Strong, strong, strong to save. Lean on my love, and know that all is well.

THE DARK PLACES   OCTOBER 8

Jesus, the very thought of Thee with Sweetness fills us.

Yes. Love me until just to think of me means joy and rapture. Gladness at the thought of One very near and dear.

It is the balm for all sorrows, the thought of me. Healing for all physical, mental and spiritual ills you can always find in thinking of me, and speaking to me.

Are doubts and fears in your hearts? Then think of me, speak to me. Instead of those fears and doubts there will flow into your hearts and beings such sweet joy as is beyond any joy of earth.

This is unfailing. Never doubt it. Courage. Courage. Courage. Fear nothing. Rejoice even in the darkest places. Rejoice.

LOVE ME MORE   OCTOBER 9

Jesus, our Lord, we Thee adore. Oh, make us love Thee more and more.

Yes! I would draw you closer and closer to me by bonds of love. The love of the sinner for the Savior, of the rescued for the rescuer, of the sheep for the loving Shepherd, of the child for its Father.

So many ties of love there are to bind you to me.

Each experience in your life of joy, and sorrow, of difficulty or success, of hardship or ease, of danger or safety, each makes its own particular demand upon me. Each serves to answer the prayer: "Make me love Thee more and more."

EXTRA WORK   OCTOBER 10

Our Lord and our God. Help us through poverty to plenty. Through unrest to rest, through sorrow to joy, through weakness to power.

I am your helper. At the end of your present path lie all these blessings. So trust and know that I am leading you.

Step with a firm step of confidence in me into each unknown day. Take every duty and every interruption as of my appointment.

You are my servant. Serve me as simply, cheerfully and readily as you expect others to serve you.

Do you blame the servant who avoids extra work, who complains about being called from one task to do one less liked? Do you feel you are ill served by such an one?

Then what of me? Is not that how you so often serve me? Think of this. Lay it to heart and view your day's work in this light.

SHAME AND DISTRESS   OCTOBER 11

I will bless the Lord at all times. His praise shall continually be in my mouth.

I sought the Lord, and he heard me, and delivered me from all my fears.

They looked unto him, and were lightened: and their faces were not ashamed.   (Psalm xxxiv. 1, 4, 5)

See, my children, that even in distress, the first step is *praise*. Before you cry in your distress, bless the Lord; even when troubles seem to overwhelm you.

That is my divine order of approach. Observe this always. In the greatest distress, search until you find cause for thankfulness. Then bless and thank.

You have thus established a line of communication between your-self and me. Along that line let your cry of distress follow.

Thus you will find I do my part, and deliverance will be sure. Oh! The gladness of heart. Lightened you will be, the burden rolled away, as the result of looking to me.

The shame and distress will be lifted too. That is always the *second* step. First right with me, and then you will be righted too in the eyes of men.

You Are My Joy   October 12

Thine they were, and Thou gavest them me and they have kept my Word.   (John xvii. 6)

Remember, that just as you thank God for me, so I thank God for his gift to me of you. In that hour of my agony on earth, one note of joy thrilled through the pain. The thought of the souls, given me by my Father, who had kept my Word.

They had not then done great deeds, as they did later, for, and in, my name. They were simple doers of my Word, not hearers only. Just in their daily tasks and ways they kept my Word.

You, too, can bring joy to my heart by faithful service. Faithful service in the little things. Be faithful.

Do your simple tasks for me.

The Sculptor's Skill   October 13

Lord, we believe, help Thou our unbelief. Lord, hear our prayers and let our cries come unto Thee.

Along the road of praise, as I told you. Yes! I will indeed help your unbelief, and in answer to your prayers grant you so great a faith, such an increasingly great faith, that each day you may look back, from the place of your larger vision, and see the faith of the day before as almost unbelief.

The beauty of my kingdom is its growth. In that kingdom there is always progress, a going on from strength to strength, from glory to glory. Be in my kingdom, and of my kingdom, and there can be no stagnation. Eternal life, abundant life is promised to all in it, and of it.

No misspent time over failures and shortcomings. Count the lessons learnt from them but as rungs in the ladder. Step up, and then cast away all thought of the manner of the making of the rung. Fashioned of joy or sorrow, of failure or success, of wounds or healing balm, what matter, my children, so long as it served its purpose?

Learn another lesson. The sculptor who finds a faulty marble casts it aside. Because it has no fashioning, it may regard itself as perfect; and it may look with scorn upon the marble the sculptor is cutting and shaping into perfection. From this, my children, learn a lesson for your lives.

THE SACRIFICE   OCTOBER 14

Behold, the Lamb of God that taketh away the sins of the world.

(John i. 29)

"Christ our Passover is sacrificed for us." I am the Lamb of God. Lay upon me your sins, your failures, your shortcomings. My sacrifice has atoned for all. I am the mediator between God and Man, the man Christ Jesus.

Do not dwell upon the past. You make my sacrifice of no effect.

No! Realize that in me you have all, complete forgiveness, complete companionship, complete healing.

FEEL PLENTY   OCTOBER 15

Live in my secret place and there the feeling is one of full satisfaction. You are to feel plenty. The storehouses of God are full to overflowing, but you must see this in your mind.

Be sure of this before you can realize it in material form.

Think thoughts of plenty. See yourselves as daughters of a king. I have told you this. Wish plenty for yourselves, and all you care for and long to help.

THE IMPRISONED GOD OCTOBER 16

Our Lord, we praise Thee and bless Thy name forever.

Yes! Praise. That moment, in the most difficult place, your sorrow is turned to joy, your fret to praise, the outward circumstances change from those of disorder to order, of chaos to calm.

The beginning of all reform must be in yourselves. However restricted your circumstances, however little you may be able to remedy financial affairs, you can always turn to yourselves, and seeing something not in order there, seek to right that.

As all reform is from within out, you will always find the outward has improved too. To do this is to release the imprisoned God—power within you.

That power, once operative, will immediately perform miracles. Then indeed shall your mourning be turned into joy.

FAITH-VISION OCTOBER 17

Turn your eyes to behold me. Look away from sordid surroundings, from lack of beauty, from the imperfections in yourselves and those around you. Then you who have the faith-vision will see all you could and do desire in me.

In your unrest behold my calm, my rest. In your impatience, my unfailing patience. In your lack and limitation, my perfection.

Looking at me you will grow like me, until men say to you, too, that you have been with Jesus.

As you grow like me you will be enabled to do the things I do, and greater works than these shall ye do because I go unto my Father.

From that place of abiding, limited by none of humanity's limitations, I can endue you with the all-conquering, all miracle-working power of your divine brother and ally.

LONELINESS OCTOBER 18

And they all forsook him and fled. (Mark xiv. 50)

Down through the ages all the simple acts of steadfast devotion, of obedience in difficulty, of loving service, have been taken by

me as an atonement for the loneliness my humanity suffered by
that desertion.

Yet I, who had realized to the full the longing of the Father to
save, and his rejection by men, the misunderstanding of his mind
and purpose, how could I think that I should not know that desertion too?

Learn, my children, from these words two lessons. Learn first that
I know what loneliness, desertion and solitude mean. Learn that every
act of yours of faithfulness is a comfort to my heart. Learn too that it
was to those deserters I gave the task of bringing my Message to mankind. To those deserters, those fearful ones, I gave my power to heal,
to raise to life.

Earth's successes are not the ones I use for the great work of my
kingdom. "They all forsook him and fled." Learn my tender understanding and pardon of human frailty. Not until man has failed has
he learnt true humility. And it is only the humble who can inherit
the earth.

HEAR MY ANSWER   OCTOBER 19

Lord, hear our prayer, and let our cry come unto Thee.

The cry of the human soul is never unheard. It is never that God does
not hear the cry, but that man fails to hear the response.

Like parts of a machine, made to fit each into the other, and to
work in perfect harmony, so is the human cry and the God-response.

But man treats this cry as if it were a thing alone, to be heard, or
not, as it pleased God, not realizing that the response was there in all
eternity, awaiting the cry, and only man's failing to heed, or to listen,
kept him unaware of the response, and unsaved, unhelped by it.

NO BURDEN IRKS   OCTOBER 20

Our Lord and our God. Be it done unto us according to Thy Word.

Simple acceptance of my will is the key to divine revelation. It will
result in both holiness and happiness. The way to the cross may be a
way of sorrow, but at its foot the burdens of sin and earth-desire are
rolled away.

The yoke of my acceptance of my Father's will in all things is adjusted to my servants' shoulders, and from that moment no burden irks or presses.

But not only in the great decisions of life accept and welcome my will. Try to see in each interruption, each task, however small, the same fulfillment of divine intent.

Accept it, say your thanks for it. Do so until this becomes a habit, and the resulting joy will transfigure and transform your lives.

A LOVE FEAST   OCTOBER 21

Behold, I stand at the door, and knock: if any man hear my voice, and open the door, I will come in to him and will sup with him, and he with me. (Rev. iii. 20)

See, my children, the knocking rests upon no merit of yours—though it is in response to the longing of your heart for me.

Keep, keep that listening ear. "If any man will hear my voice." Again no merit of yours. Only the ear bent to catch my tones, and to hear the sound of my gentle knocking.

Then listen: "If any man hear my voice, and open the door, I will come in to him, and will sup with him, and he with me."

What a feast! You think it would have been joy to have been present at the Marriage feast of Cana of Galilee, or to have been one of my disciples in the upper room, seated with me at the Last Supper or one of the two at Emmaus, or one of the few for whom I prepared that lakeside feast!

But oh! At each of these feasts, God-provided and God-companioned as they were, you could not have known the rapture you may know as you hear the knocking and the voice, and, opening, bid me welcome to my feast.

A feast of tenderest companionship, of divine Sustenance, truly a love feast.

HOME-BUILDING   OCTOBER 22

You are building up an unshakable faith. Be furnishing the quiet places of your souls now.

Fill them with all that is harmonious and good, beautiful and enduring.

Home-build in the Spirit now, and the waiting time will be well spent.

HILL OF SACRIFICE   OCTOBER 23

You must trust to the end. You must be ready to go on trusting to the last hour.

You must *know* even when you cannot *see*. . . . You must be ready, like my servant Abraham, to climb the very hill of sacrifice, to go to the very last moment, before you see my deliverance.

This final test has to come to all who walk by faith. You must rely on me *alone*.

Look to no other arm, look for no other help. Trust in the Spirit Forces of the unseen, not in those you see. Trust and fear not.

SALT OF EARTH   OCTOBER 24

Our Lord, we bless Thee and thank Thee for Thy keeping power.

Yes! "Kept by the power of God" is a promise, and an assurance that holds joy and beauty for the believing soul.

The keeping that means security, safety, is wonderful. There is, too, the keeping that implies life, freshness, purity, the being "kept unspotted from the world."

Then there is the keeping that I ensure to those of whom I speak as the salt of the earth.

"Ye are the salt of the earth: but if the salt have lost his savor it is henceforth good for nothing, but to be cast out, and to be trodden under foot of men."

Only in very close contact with me is the keeping power realized. That keeping power which maintains the salt at its freshest and best, and also preserves from corruption that portion of the world in which I place it.

What a work! Not by activity in this case, but simply by its existing, by its quality.

No Unemployment OCTOBER 25

The way of conquest over the material, the temporal, which all my disciples should know, is learned by the conquest of the physical, the self-life, in each of you.

So seek, in all things, to conquer. Take this as a very definite guidance. Circumstances are adverse. Temporal power, as money, needs to be forthcoming.

Then seek daily more and more to obtain this self-conquest, and you are gaining surely, though you may not see it, conquest over the temporal forces and powers.

Unemployment would cease if man realized this.

If he has not the work let him make himself a conquering force, beginning with the conquest of all evil in himself, then in his home, then in all round him. He will have become a force that will be needed, and *must* be employed.

There are no idle hours in my kingdom. Waiting may seem a time of inactivity, as far as the outer world is concerned, but it can, and should, be a time of great activity in the inner life, and the surrounding material plane.

Deserters OCTOBER 26

You must believe utterly. My love can bear nothing less. I am so often "wounded in the house of my friends." Do you think the spitting and scorn of my enemies, the mocking and reviling hurt me? No!

"They all forsook him and fled." "I know not the man." These left their scars.

So now, it is not the unbelief of my enemies that hurts, but that my friends, who love and know me, cannot walk all the way with me, and doubt my power to do all that I have said.

Days of Conquest OCTOBER 27

I see the loving, striving, not the defects. I see the conquest of your particular battle. I count it victory, a glad victory.

I do not compare it with the strenuous campaigns of my great saints.

For you it is victory, and the angels rejoice, and your dear ones rejoice, as much as at any conquest noted, and rejoiced over, by heaven.

My children, count the days of conquest as very blessed days.

GLAD SURPRISES   OCTOBER 28

Our Lord, we know that all is well. We trust Thee for all. We love Thee increasingly. We bow to Thy will.

Bow not as one who is resigned to some heavy blow about to fall or to the acceptance of some inevitable decision.

Bow as a child bows, in anticipation of a glad surprise being prepared for it by one who loves it.

Bow in *such* a way, just waiting to hear the loving word to raise your head, and see the glory and joy and wonder of your surprise.

DISCOUNT MONEY   OCTOBER 29

Never count success by money gained. That is not the mind of my kingdom. Your success is the measure of my will and mind that you have revealed to those around you.

Your success is the measure of my will that those around you have seen worked out in your lives.

THE HARDEST LESSON   OCTOBER 30

Wait and you shall realize the joy of the one who can be calm and wait, knowing that all is well. The last, and hardest lesson, is that of waiting. So wait.

I would almost say tonight "forgive me, children, that I allow this extra burden to rest upon you even for so short a time."

I would have you know this, that from the moment you placed all in my hands, and sought no other aid, from that moment I have taken the quickest way possible to work out your salvation, and to free you.

There is so much you have had to be taught—to avoid future disaster. But the friend with whom you stand by the grave of failure, of dead ambitions, of relinquished desires, that friend is a friend for all time.

Use this waiting time to cement the friendship with me, and to increase your knowledge of me.

THE VOICE AGAIN   OCTOBER 31

Thy Word is a lamp unto our feet and a light unto our path.

(Psalm cxix. 105)

Yes! My Word, the Scriptures. Read them, study them, store them in your hearts, use them as you use a lamp to guide your footsteps.

But remember, my children, my Word is more even than that. It is the voice that speaks to your hearts, that inner consciousness that tells of me.

It is the voice that speaks to you intimately, personally, in this sacred evening time. It is even more than that. It is I your Lord and friend.

"And the Word was made flesh and dwelt among us." Truly a lamp to your feet, and a light to your path.

NOVEMBER

PRAYER OF JOY

Joy is the messenger, dear Lord, that bears our prayers to Thee.

Prayer can be like incense, rising ever higher and higher, or it can be like a low earth-mist clinging to the ground, never once soaring.

The eye that sees all, the ear that hears all, knows *every* cry.

But the prayer of real faith is the prayer of joy, that sees and knows the heart of love it rises to greet, and that is so sure of a glad response.

SPEND

Give, give, give. Keep ever an empty vessel for me to fill.

In future use all for me, and give all *you* cannot use.

How poor die those who leave wealth! Wealth is to use, to spend, for me.

Use as you go. Delight to use.

NO LIMIT

Unlimited supply, that is my law. Oh! The unlimited supply, and oh! The poor, blocked channels! Will you feel this, that there is no limit to my power?

But man asks, and blasphemes in asking, such poor mean things. Do you not see how you wrong me? I desire to give you a gift, and if you are content with the poor, and the mean, and the sordid, then you are insulting me, the giver.

"Ask what ye will and it shall be done unto you." How I can fulfill the promise is my work, not yours, to consider. . . . Have a big faith, and expect big things, and you will get big things.

I AM BESIDE YOU   NOVEMBER 4

In Thy presence is fullness of joy; at Thy right hand there are pleasures
for evermore. (Psalm xvi. 11)

Do not seek to realize this fullness of joy as the result of effort. This cannot be, any more than joy in a human friend's presence would come as the result of trying to force yourself to like to have that friend with you.

Call often my name, "Jesus."

The calling of my name does not really summon me. I am beside you. But it removes, as it were, the scales from your eyes, and you see me.

It is, as it were, the pressure of a loved one's hand, that brings an answering pressure, and a thrill of joy follows, a real, and a joyful sense of nearness.

SECOND ADVENT   NOVEMBER 5

Jesus, comforter of all the sorrowing, help us to bring Thy comfort into
every heart and life to which Thou art longing to express that comfort
through us. Use us, Lord. The years may be many or few. Place us
where we can best serve Thee, and influence most for Thee.

The world would be brought to me so soon, so soon, if only all who acknowledge me as Lord, as Christ, gave themselves unreservedly to be used by me.

I could use *each* human body as mightily as I used my own human body as a channel for divine love and power.

I do not delay my second coming. My *followers* delay it.

If each lived for me, by me, in me, allowing me to live in him, to use him to express the divine through him, as I expressed it when on earth, then long ago the world would have been drawn to me, and I should have come to claim my own.

So seek, my children, to live, knowing no other desire but to express me, and to show my love to your world.

GOD IN ACTION   NOVEMBER 6

Power is not such an overwhelming force as it sounds, a something you call to your aid, to intervene in crises. No! *Power is just God in action.*

Therefore whenever a servant of mine, however weak he humanly may be, allows God to work through him, then all he does is *powerful.*

Carry this thought with you through the days in which you seem to accomplish little. Try to see it is not you, but the divine Spirit in you. All you have to do, as I have told you before, is to turn self out. A very powerful axe in a master hand accomplishes much. The same in the hand of a weak child, nothing. So see that it is not the instrument, but the master hand that wields the instrument, that tells.

Remember no day is lost on which some spiritual truth becomes clearer. No day is lost which you have given to me to use. My use of it may not have been apparent to you. Leave that to me. Dwell in me, and I in you, so shall ye bear much fruit. The fruit is not the work of the branches, though proudly the branches may bear it. It is the work of the vine, that sends its life-giving sap through those branches. I am the vine and ye are the branches.

SELF KILLS POWER   NOVEMBER 7

Dwelling with me, desiring only my will and to do my work, my Spirit cannot fail to pass through the channel of your life into the lives of others.

Many think it is humility to say they do little, and are of little value to my world. To think *that* is pride.

What if the pipe were to say "I do so little, I wish I could be more use." The reply would be "It is not you, but the water that passes through you, that saves and blesses. All you have to do is to see there is nothing to block the way so that the water cannot flow through."

The only block there can be in *your* channel is self. Keep that out, and know that my Spirit is flowing through. Therefore all must be the better for coming in contact with both of you, because you are channels. See this, and you will think it natural to know they are being helped, not by you, but by my Spirit flowing through you as a channel.

WIPE THE SLATE   NOVEMBER 8

One thing I do, forgetting those things which are behind, and reaching forth unto those things which are before, I press toward the mark.
(Phil. iii. 13)

Forget the past. Remember only its glad days. Wipe the slate of your remembrance with love, which will erase all that is not confirmed in love. You must forget your failures, *your* failures and those of others. Wipe them out of the book of your remembrance.

I did not die upon the cross for man to bear the burdens of his sins himself. "Who his own self bare our sins in his own body on the tree."

If you forget not the sins of others, and I bear them, then you add to my sorrows.

WONDERFUL FRIENDSHIP   NOVEMBER 9

Think of me as a friend, but realize, too, the wonder of the friendship. As soon as man gives me not only worship and honor, obedience, allegiance, but loving understanding, then he becomes my friend, even as I am his.

What I can do for you. Yes! But also what we can do for each other. What you can do for me.

Your service becomes so different when you feel I count on your great friendship to do this or that for me. . . .

Dwell more, dwell much, on this thought of you as my friends, and of the sweetness of my knowing where I can turn for love, for understanding, for help.

NEW FORCES   NOVEMBER 10

Remember that life's difficulties and troubles are not intended to arrest your progress, but to increase your speed. You must call new forces, new powers into action.

Whatever it is must be surmounted, overcome. Remember this. It is as a race. Nothing must daunt you. Do not let a difficulty conquer you. You must conquer it.

My strength will be there awaiting you. Bring all your thought, all your power, into action. Nothing is too *small* to be faced and overcome. To push small difficulties aside is to be preparing big troubles.

Rise to conquer. It is the path of victory I would have you tread. There can be no failure with me.

"Now unto him that is able to keep you from falling, and to present you faultless before the presence of his glory with exceeding joy. . . ."

HEAVEN'S COLORS   NOVEMBER 11

Looking back you will see that every step was planned. Leave all to me. Each stone in the mosaic fits into the perfect pattern, designed by the master Artist.

It is all so wonderful!

But the colors are of heaven's hues, so that your eyes could not bear to gaze on the whole, until you are beyond the veil.

So, stone by stone, you see, and trust the pattern to the designer.

THE VOICELESS CRY   NOVEMBER 12

Jesus, hear us, and let our cry come unto Thee.

That voiceless cry, that comes from anguished hearts, is heard above all the music of heaven.

It is not the arguments of theologians that solve the problems of a questioning heart, but the cry of that heart to me, and the certainty that I have heard.

EVERY PROBLEM SOLVED   NOVEMBER 13

Man has such strange ideas of the meaning of my invitation "Come unto me." Too often has it been interpreted as an urge to pay a duty owed to a Creator, or a debt owed to a Savior.

The "Come unto me" holds in it a wealth of meaning far surpassing even that. "Come unto me" for the solution of every problem, for the calming of every fear, for all you need—physical, mental, spiritual.

Sick, come to me for health. Homeless, ask me for a home. friendless, claim a friend. Hopeless, a refuge.

"Come unto me" for everything.

DEVIOUS WAYS   NOVEMBER 14

Life is not easy, my children. Man has made of it not what my Father meant it to be.

Ways that were meant to be straight paths have been made by man into ways devious and evil, filled with obstacles and stones of difficulty.

BY MY SPIRIT   NOVEMBER 15

Man is apt to think that once in time only was my miracle-working power in action. That is not so. Wherever man trusts wholly in me, and leaves to me the choosing of the very day and hour, then there is my miracle-working power as manifest, as marvelously manifest today, as ever it was when I was on earth, as ever it was to set my apostles free, or to work miracles of wonder and healing through them.

Trust in me. Have a boundless faith in me, and you will see, and, seeing, will give me all the glory. Remember, and say often to yourselves, "not by might, nor by power, but by my Spirit, saith the Lord."

Dwell much in thought upon all I accomplished on earth, and then say to yourselves "he, our Lord, our friend, could accomplish this now in our lives."

Apply these miracles to your present day need, and know that your help and salvation are sure.

UNION IS POWER   NOVEMBER 16

Where two or three are gathered together in my name there am I in the midst of them.   (Matt. xviii. 20)

Claim that promise always. Know it true that when two of my lovers meet I am the Third. Never limit that promise.

When you two are together in my name, united by one bond in my Spirit, I am there. Not only when you meet to greet me, and to hear my voice.

Think what this means in power. It is again the lesson of the power that follows *two united to serve me.*

QUIET LIVES   NOVEMBER 17

Well done, thou good and faithful servant. Enter thou into the joy of thy Lord.   (Matt. xxv. 2)

These words are whispered in the ears of many whom the world would pass by unrecognizing. Not to the great, and the world-famed, are these words said so often, but to the quiet followers who serve me unobtrusively, yet faithfully, who bear their cross bravely, with a smiling face to the world. Thank me for the quiet lives.

These words speak not only of the passing into that fuller Spirit life. Duty faithfully done for me does mean entrance into a life of joy—my joy, the joy of your Lord. The world may never see it, the humble, patient, quiet service, but I see it, and my reward is not earth's fame, earth's wealth, earth's pleasures, but the joy divine.

Whether here, or there, in the earth-world, or in the spirit-world, this is my reward. Joy. The joy that carries an exquisite thrill in the midst of pain and poverty and suffering. That joy of which I said no man could take it from you. Earth has no pleasure, no reward, that can give man *that* joy. It is known only to my lovers and my friends.

This joy may come, not as the reward of activity in my service. It may be the reward of patient suffering, bravely borne.

Suffering, borne with me, must in time bring joy, as does all real contact with me. So live with me in that kingdom of joy, my kingdom, the gateway into which may be *service,* it may be *suffering.*

DAZZLING GLORY   NOVEMBER 18

Arise, shine, for thy light is come, and the glory of the Lord is risen upon thee.   (Isa. lx. 1)

The glory of the Lord is the beauty of his character. It is risen upon you when you realize it, even though on earth you can do so only in part.

The beauty of the purity and love of God is too dazzling for mortals to see in full.

The glory of the Lord is also risen upon yon when you reflect that glory in your lives, when in love, patience, service, purity, whatever it may be, you reveal to the world a something of the Father, an assurance that you have been with me, your Lord and Savior.

HILLS OF THE LORD   NOVEMBER 19

I will lift up mine eyes unto the hills, from whence cometh my help. My help cometh from the Lord, which made heaven and earth.

(Psalm cxxi. 1, 2)

Yes! Always raise your eyes, from earth's sordid and mean and false, to the hills of the Lord. From poverty, lift your eyes to the help of the Lord.

In moments of weakness, lift your eyes to the hills of the Lord.

Train your sight by constantly getting this long view. Train it to see more and more, further and further, until distant peaks seem familiar.

The hills of the Lord. The hills whence comes your help. A parched earth looks to the hills for its rivers, its streams, its life. So look you to the hills. From those hills comes help. Help from the Lord—who made heaven and earth.

So, for all your spiritual needs, look to the Lord, who made heaven, and for all your temporal needs look to me, owner of all this, the Lord who made the earth.

MYSTERIES   NOVEMBER 20

Your hope is in the Lord. More and more set your hopes on me. Know that whatever the future may hold it will hold more and more of me. It cannot but be glad and full of joy. So in heaven, or on earth, wherever you may be, your way must be truly one of delight.

Do not try to find answers to the mysteries of the world. Learn to know me more and more, and in that knowledge you will have all the answers you need here, and when you see me face to face, in that purely spiritual world, you will find no need to ask. There again all your answers will be in me.

Remember, I was the answer in time to all man's questions about my Father and his laws. Know no theology. Know me. I was the Word of God. All you need to know about God you know in me. If a man knows me not, all your explanations will fall on an unresponsive heart.

RADIATE JOY   NOVEMBER 21

Not only must you rejoice, but your joy must be made manifest. "Known unto all men." A candle must not be set under a bushel, but on a candlestick, that it may give light to all who are in the house.

Men must see and know your joy, and seeing it, know, without any doubt, that it springs from trust in me, from living with me.

The hard dull way of resignation is not *my* way. When I entered Jerusalem, knowing well that scorn and reviling and death awaited me, it was with cries of Hosanna, and with a triumphal procession. Not just a few "Lost Cause" followers creeping with me into the city. There was no note of sadness in my Last Supper Talk with my disciples, and "when we had sung an hymn" we went out unto the Mount of Olives.

So trust, so conquer, so joy. Love colors the way. Love takes the sting out of the wind of adversity.

Love. Love. Love of me. The consciousness of my presence, and that of my Father, we are one, and he—God—is love.

ONLY LOVE LASTS   NOVEMBER 22

Though I speak with the tongues of men and of angels, and have not charity, I am become as sounding brass, or a tinkling cymbal.

(1 Cor. xiii. 1)

See that only love tells. Only what is done in love lasts, for God is love, and only the work of God remains.

The fame of the world, the applause given to the one who speaks with the tongues of men and of angels, who attracts admiration and compels attention, it is all given to what is passing, is really worthless, if it lacks that God-quality, love.

Think how a smile, or word of love, goes winged on its way, a God-power, simple though it may seem, while the mighty words of an orator can fall fruitless to the ground. The test of all true work and words is—are they inspired by love?

If man only saw how vain is so much of his activity! So much work done in my name is not acknowledged by me. Ask for love. Turn out from your hearts and lives all that is not loving, so shall ye bear much fruit, and by this shall all men know ye are my disciples, because ye have love one toward another.

EARTH'S FURIES   NOVEMBER 23

In the world ye shall have tribulation: but be of good cheer! I have over-come the world.   (John xvi. 33)

Then you may ask why have you, my children, to have tribulation if I have overcome the world.

My overcoming was never, you know, for myself, but for you, for my children. Each temptation, each difficulty, I overcame as it presented itself.

The powers of evil were strained to their utmost to devise means to break me. They failed, but how they failed was known only to me, and to my Father, who could read my undaunted spirit. The world, even my own followers, would see a Lost Cause. Reviled, spat upon, scourged, they would deem me conquered. How could they know my Spirit was free, unbroken, unharmed?

And so, as I had come to show man God, I must show him God unconquered, unharmed, untouched by evil and its power. *Man* could not see my Spirit untouched, risen above these earth furies and hates, into the secret place of the Father. But man could see my risen body, and learn by that, that even the last attempt of man had been powerless to touch me.

Take heart from that, for you must share my tribulations. If evil is to leave you unchallenged you must be evil. If evil challenges you, if trials press sore, it is because you are on my side, and, as my friends, exposed to the hate of evil.

But be of good cheer. You walk with me. I conquered evil at every point, though man could only see it proved beyond all doubt when I rose from the dead. And in *my* conquering power you walk unharmed today.

SUFFER TO SAVE   NOVEMBER 24

Take each day's happenings as work you can do for me. In that Spirit a blessing will attend all you do. Offering your day's service thus to me, you are sharing in my lifework, and therefore helping me to save my world.

You may not see it, but the power of vicarious sacrifice is redemptive beyond man's power of understanding here on earth.

THE HEAVENLY BEGGAR   NOVEMBER 25

Behold, I stand at the door and knock.   (Rev. iii. 20)

Oh, ponder again these words and learn from them my great humility.

There is that gracious invitation, too, for those who yearn to realize a happiness, a rest, a satisfaction they have never found in the world and its pursuits. To them the pleading answer to their quest is "Come to me and I will give you rest."

But to those who do not feel their need of me, who obstinately reject me, who shut the doors of their hearts so that I may not enter, to these I go, in tender, humble longing. Even when I find all closed, all barred, I stand a Beggar, knocking, knocking. The heavenly beggar in his great humility.

Never think of those who have shut you out, or forgotten you, that now they must wait, you have no need of them. No! Remember *that,* the heavenly beggar, and learn of me, humility.

Learn too the value of each man's happiness, and peace and rest, to me, his God; and learn, and learning pray to copy, the divine unrest until a soul finds rest and peace in me.

MY BEAUTY   NOVEMBER 26

The prophet realized the truth of my later saying "he that hath ears to hear let him hear," which might be rendered "he that hath eyes to see let him see."

The God who was to be born upon earth was not to be housed in a body so beautiful that men would follow and adore for the beauty of his countenance.

No! He was to be as one whom the world would despise, but, to the seeing eye, the Spirit that dwelt in that body should be so beautiful as to lack nothing. "Yet when we shall see him, there is no beauty that we should desire him."

Pray for the seeing eye, to see the beauty of my character, of my Spirit. Nay, more, as faith saw the beauty of the Godhead in One who had no form or comeliness, so pray to have that faith to see the beauty of my love in my dealings with you, in my actions. Till, in what the world will distort into cruelty and harshness, you, with the eyes of faith, will see all that you could desire.

Know me. Talk to me. Let me talk to you, so that I may make clear to your loving hearts what seems mysterious now and purposeless ("having no form nor comeliness").

NOT THWARTED   NOVEMBER 27

Not our wills but Thine, O Lord.

Man has so misunderstood me in this. I want no will laid grudgingly upon my Altar. I want you to desire and love my will, because therein lies your happiness and Spirit-rest.

Whenever you feel that you cannot leave the choice to me then pray, not to be able to accept my will, but to know and love me more. With that knowledge, and the love, will come the certainty that I know best, and that I want only the best for you and yours.

How little those know me who think I wish to thwart them. How often I am answering their own prayers in the best and quickest way.

The Way of the Spirit   NOVEMBER 28

Jesus, we come to Thee with joy.

The joy of meeting me should more and more fill your lives. It will. Your lives must first of all be narrowed down, more and more, into an inner circle life with me (the three of us), and then, as that friendship becomes more and more engrossing, more and more binding, then, gradually, the circle of your interests will widen.

For the present do not think of it as a narrow life. I have my purpose, my loving purpose, in cutting you away from other work and interests, for the time.

To work from large interests and a desire for great activities and world movements, to the inner circle life with me, is really the wrong way. That is why so often, when, through all these activities and interests, a soul finds me, I have to begin our friendship by cutting away the ties that bind it to the outer and wider circle. When it has gained strength and learned its lesson in the inner circle it can then widen its life, working this time from within out, taking then to each contact, each friendship, the inner circle influence.

And this is to be your way of life.

This is the way of the Spirit. Man so often misunderstands this.

When Two Agree   NOVEMBER 29

If two of you shall agree.

I am the truth. Every word of mine is true. Every promise of mine shall be fulfilled.

First, "gathered together in my name," bound by a common loyalty to me, desirous only of doing my will.

Then, when this is so, I am present too, a self-invited guest, and when I am there and one with you, voicing the same petition, making your demands mine, then it follows the request is granted.

But what man has failed perhaps to realize is *all* that lies behind the words. For two to agree about the wisdom of a request, to be certain it *should* be granted, and will be granted (if it should be), is not the same as two agreeing to pray that request.

FROM SELF TO GOD   NOVEMBER 30

The eternal God is thy refuge.   (Deut. xxxiii. 27)

A place to flee to, a sanctuary. An escape from misunderstanding, *from yourself.* You can get away from others into the quiet of your own being, but from yourself, from the sense of your failure, your weakness, your sins and shortcomings, whither can you flee?

To the eternal God your refuge. Till in his immensity you forget your smallness, meanness, limitations.

Till the relief of safety merges into joy of appreciation of your refuge, and you absorb the divine, and absorbing gain strength to conquer.

December

Responsibility December 1

I am beside you. A very human Jesus, who understands all your weaknesses, and sees too your struggles and conquests.

Remember, I was the companion of the weak. Ready to supply their hunger. Teaching my followers their responsibility towards all, not only those near and dear to them, but to the multitude.

"Lord, send them away that they may go into the villages and buy themselves victuals," said my disciples, with no sympathy for the fainting, exhausted men, women and children.

But I taught that divine Sympathy includes responsibility. "Give ye them to eat," was my reply. I taught that pity, without a remedy for the evil, or the need, is worthless.

"Give ye them to eat." Wherever your sympathy goes, you must go too, if possible. Remember *that* in thinking of your own needs. Claim from me the same attitude now.

The servant is not above his master, certainly not in spiritual attainments, and what I taught my disciples, *I* do.

So fainting and needy, by the lakeside of life, know that I will supply your need, not grudgingly, but in full measure.

The Ideal Man December 2

Draw nigh, shoes off thy feet, in silent awe and adoration. Draw nigh, as Moses drew near to the burning bush.

I give you the loving intimacy of a friend, but I am God too, and the wonder of our intercourse, the miracle of your intimacy with me, will mean the more to you, if sometimes you see the majestic figure of the Son of God.

Draw nigh in the utter confidence that is the sublimest prayer. Draw nigh. No far-off pleading, even to a God clothed with majesty of fire. Draw nigh. Draw nigh, not as a suppliant, but as a listener. I am the Suppliant, as I make known to you my wishes. For this majestic God is brother too, longing so intensely that you should serve your brother-man, and longing, even more intensely, that you should be true to that vision he has of you.

You speak of your fellow man as disappointing you, as falling short of the ideal you had of him. But what of me? For every man there is the ideal man I see in him. The man he could be, the man I would have him be.

Judge of my heart when he fails to fulfill that promise. The disappointments of man may be great and many, they are nothing as compared with my disappointments. Remember this, and strive to be the friend I see in my vision of you.

A Journey With Me   December 3

Fret not your souls with puzzles that you cannot solve. The solution may never be shown you until you have left this flesh-life.

Remember what I have so often told you, "I have yet many things to say unto you, but ye cannot bear them now." Only step by step, and stage by stage, can you proceed, in your journey upward.

The one thing to be sure of is, that it is a journey with me. There does come a joy known to those who suffer with me. But that is not the result of the suffering, but the result of the close intimacy with me, to which suffering drove you.

Man of Sorrows   December 4

He is despised and rejected of men; a man of sorrows, and acquainted with grief: and we hid as it were our faces from him; he was despised, end we esteemed him not. (Isa. liii. 3)

That these words strike a note of beauty in the hearts of those attuned to hear the beautiful, shows truly that the heart recognizes the need for the Man of *Sorrows*. That it sees nothing contemptible in One despised by the world. That it recognizes the vast difference between the values of heaven, and those of the world. Fame and acclamations are accorded to earth's great, contempt and rejection to the Son of God.

One of the things my disciples must ever seek to do, is to set aside the valuation of the world, and judge only according to the values of heaven. Do not seek the praise and the notice of men. These are not for you. You follow a despised Christ. See the mob is hooting, throwing stones, jeering, and yet in that quiet little throng there is a happiness and joy the reviling crowds could never know.

Follow that little throng with stones and gibes, and it appears to be of men, mean, ludicrous, contemptible. Be one of the throng, and you feel the majesty of God in the presence of him, Who was despised and rejected of men. Wreaths around his brow, and shouts of applause, would belittle that majesty.

In your dark hours, when human help fails, keep very close to the Man of Sorrows. Feel my hand of love press yours in silent but complete understanding. I, too, was acquainted with grief. No heart can ache without my heart aching too. "He was despised, and we esteemed him not."

LAW OF SUPPLY   DECEMBER 5

The first law of giving is of the spirit world. Give to all you meet, or whose lives touch yours, of your prayers, your time, yourselves, your love, your thought. You must practice *this* giving first.

Then give of this world's goods and money, as you have them given to you. To give money and material things, without having first made the habit daily, hourly, ever increasingly, of giving on the higher plane, is wrong.

Give, give, give all your best to all who need it. Be great givers—great givers. Give as I said my Father in heaven gives. He who makes his sun to shine on the evil and on the good, and sendeth rain on the just and on the unjust. Remember, as I have told you before, give according to need, never according to desert. In giving, with the thought of supplying a real need you most closely resemble that Father in heaven, the great giver.

As you receive, you must supply the needs of those I bring to you. Not questioning, not limiting. Their nearness to you, their relationship, must never count. Only their need is to guide you. Pray to become great givers.

EXPECT TEMPTATION   DECEMBER 6

Lord, give us power to conquer temptation as Thou didst in the wilderness.

The very first step towards conquering temptation is to see it as temptation. To dissociate yourself from it.

Not to think of it as a something resulting from your tiredness, or illness, or poverty, or nerve-strain, when you feel you might well excuse yourself for yielding, but first to realize very fully that when you have heard my voice ("the heavens opened," as it were) and are going to fulfill your mission to work for me and to draw souls to me, you must expect a mighty onslaught from the evil one, who will endeavor with all his might to frustrate you, and to prevent your good work. Expect that.

Then when these little temptations, or big ones, come, you will recognize them as planned by evil to thwart me. Then for very love of me you will conquer.

FOOD OF LIFE   DECEMBER 7

I have meat to eat that ye know not of.

Those were my words to my disciples in the early days of my ministry. Later I was to lead them on to a fuller understanding of that majestic union of a soul with God in which strength, life and food pass from One to the other.

Meat is to sustain the body. To do the will of God is the very strength and support of life. Feed on that food.

Soul-starvation comes from the failing to do, and to delight in doing, my will. How busy the world is in talking of bodies that are undernourished! What of the souls that are undernourished?

Make it indeed your meat to do my will. Strength and power will indeed come to you from that.

MY KINGDOM   DECEMBER 8

And greater works than these shall ye do, because I go unto my Father.

While I was on the earth, to the great number of those with whom I came in contact, mine was a lost cause. Even my disciples only believed, half doubting, half wondering. When they all forsook me and fled it was not so much fear of my enemies as the certainty that my mission, however beautiful they thought it, had failed.

In spite of all I had taught them, in spite of the intimate revelation of the Last Supper, they had secretly felt sure that when the final moment came, and the hatred of the Pharisees was openly declared against me I should sound some call to action, and that I should lead my many followers, and found my earthly kingdom. Even the disciples who had eyes to see my spiritual kingdom had thought material forces had proved too strong for me.

But with my Resurrection came hope. Faith revived. They would remind each other of all I had said. They would have the assurance of my divinity, Messiahship, the lack of which had hindered my work on earth, and they would have all my power in the unseen—the Holy Spirit—to help them.

Remember, I came to found a kingdom—the kingdom. Those who lived in the kingdom were to do the work—greater works than I was able to do. Not a greater power shown, not a greater life lived, but, as men recognized my Godhead, opportunities for works in my name would increase. My work on earth was to gather around me the nucleus of my kingdom, and to teach the truths of my kingdom to them. In those truths they were to live and work.

YOUR SEARCH REWARDED   DECEMBER 9

Lord, all men seek for Thee.

All men seek for me, but all men do not know what they want. They are seeking because they are dissatisfied without realizing that I am the object of their quest.

Count it your greatest joy to be the means, by your lives, sufferings, words and love, to prove to the questing ones you know that their search would end when they saw me.

Profit by my example. I left my work—seemingly the greatest work—that of saving souls, to seek communion with my Father. Did I know perhaps that with many it was idle curiosity? Did I know that there must be no rush into the kingdom, that the still small voice, not the shoutings of a mob, would alone persuade men I was the Son of God?

Why be surrounded by multitudes if the multitudes were not really desiring to learn from, and to follow, me. Follow the Christ into the quiet places of prayer.

THE QUIET TIME   DECEMBER 10

There may be many times when I reveal nothing, command nothing, give no guidance. But your path is clear, and your task, to grow daily more and more into the knowledge of me. *That* this quiet time with me will enable you to do.

I may ask you to sit silent before me, and I may speak no word that you could *write*. All the same that waiting *with* me will bring comfort and peace. Only friends who understand and love each other can wait silent in each other's presence.

And it may be that I shall prove our friendship by asking you to wait in silence while I rest with you, assured of your love and understanding. So wait, so love, so joy.

A SUNRISE GIFT   DECEMBER 11

To those whose lives have been full of struggle and care, who have felt as you both have, the tragedy of living, the pity of an agonized heart for my poor world—to those of my followers I give that peace and joy that brings to age its second spring, the youth they sacrificed for me, and for my world. . . .

Take each day now as a joyous sunrise gift from me. Your simple daily tasks done in my strength and love will bring the consciousness of all your highest hopes. Expect great things. Expect great things.

CARE-FREE   DECEMBER 12

Perfect love casteth out fear.

Love and fear cannot dwell together. By their very natures they cannot exist side by side. Evil is powerful, and fear is one of evil's most potent forces.

Therefore a weak vacillating love can be soon routed by fear, whereas a perfect love, a trusting love, is immediately the Conqueror, and fear, vanquished, flees in confusion.

But I am love because God is love, and I and the Father are one. So the only way to obtain this perfect love, that dispels fear, is to have me more and more in your lives. You can only banish fear by my presence and my name.

Fear of the future—Jesus will be with us.

Fear of poverty—Jesus will provide. (And so to all the temptations of fear.)

You must not allow fear to enter. Talk to me. Think of me. Talk of me. Love me. And that sense of my power will so possess you that no fear can possess your mind. Be strong in this my love.

PERPETUAL GUIDANCE   DECEMBER 13

Fullness of joy. The joy of perpetual guidance. The joy of knowing that every detail of your lives is planned by me, but planned with a wealth of tenderness and love.

Wait for guidance in every step. Wait to be shown my way. The thought of this loving leading should give you great joy. All the responsibility of life taken off your shoulders. All its business worry taken off your shoulders. It is indeed a joy for you to feel so free and yet so planned for.

Oh! The wonder of this—a God-guided life. To think anything impossible in such circumstances is to say it cannot be done by me. To say that is surely a denial of me.

STORMS   DECEMBER 14

Our loving Lord, we thank Thee for Thy marvelous keeping power.

There is no miracle so wonderful as the miracle of a soul being kept by my power. Forces of evil batter and storm, but are powerless. Tempests rage unavailingly.

It is like a cool garden with sweet flowers and bees and butterflies and trees and playing fountains set in the midst of a mighty roaring city. Try to see your lives as that.

Not only as calm and unmoved, but as breathing fragrance, expressing beauty. Expect storms. Know this—you cannot be united in your great friendship and bond to do my work, and in your great love for me, and not excite the envy, hatred and malice of all whom you meet who are not on my side.

Where does the enemy attack? The fortress, the stronghold, not the desert waste.

MY SHADOW   DECEMBER 15

Learn that each day must be lived in my power, and in the consciousness of my presence, even if the thrill of joy seems to be absent. Remember that if sometimes there seems a shadow on your lives—it is not the withdrawal of my presence. It is my shadow as I stand between you and your foes.

Even with your nearest and dearest there are the quiet days. You do not doubt *their* love because you do not hear their laughter, and feel a thrill of joy at their nearness.

The quiet grey days are the days for duty. Work in the calm certainty that I am with you.

WHAT JOY IS   DECEMBER 16

Lord, give us Thy joy, that joy that no man, no poverty, no circumstances, no conditions can take from us.

You shall have my joy. But life just now for you both is a march—a toilsome march. . . . The joy will come, but for the moment do not think of that, think simply of the march. Joy is the reward. . . .

Between my promise of the gift of joy to my disciples and their realization of that joy came sense of failure, disappointment, denial, desertion, hopelessness, then hope, waiting, and courage in the face of danger.

Joy is the reward of patiently seeing me in the dull dark days, of trusting when you cannot see. . . . Joy is as it were your heart's response to my smile of recognition of your faithfulness. . . .

Stop thinking your lives are all wrong if you do not feel it. . . . Remember you may not yet be joyous, but you are brave, and courage and unselfish thought for others are as sure signs of true discipleship as joy.

CONDITIONS OF BLESSING   DECEMBER 17

Jesus, we love Thee. We see that all things are planned by Thee. We rejoice in that vision.

Rejoice in the fact that you are mine. The privileges of the members of my kingdom are many. When I said of my Father "he maketh his Sun to rise on the evil and on the good, and sendeth rain on the just and on the unjust," you will notice it was of temporal and material blessings I spoke.

I did not mean that believer and unbeliever could be treated alike. That is not possible; I can send rain and sunshine and money and worldly blessings equally to both, but of the blessing of the kingdom that would be impossible.

There are conditions that control the bestowal of these. My followers do not always understand this, and it is necessary they should do so if they are remembering my injunction which followed—"Be ye therefore perfect even as your Father in heaven is perfect."

To attempt to bestow on all alike your love and understanding and interchange of thought would be impossible. But temporal blessings you too bestow, as does my Father. All must be done in love and in the spirit of true forgiveness.

SEE WONDERS   DECEMBER 18

Think your thought-way into the very heart of my kingdom. See there the abundance of delights in my storehouse, and lay eager hands on them.

See wonders, ask wonders, bear wonders away with you. Remember this beautiful earth on which you are was once only a thought of divine mind. Think how from your thought one corner of it could grow and become a garden of the Lord, a Bethany home for your master, a place to which I have a right to bring my friends, my needy ones, for talk and rest with me.

PERFECT LOVE   DECEMBER 19

Our Lord, give us that Perfect love of Thee that casts out all fear.

Never let yourselves fear anybody or anything. No fear of my failing you. No fear that your faith will fail you. No fear of poverty or loneliness. No fear of not knowing the way. No fear of others. No fear of their misunderstanding.

But, my children, this absolute casting out of fear is the result of a Perfect love, a perfect love of me and my Father. Speak to me about everything. Listen to me at all times. Feel my tender nearness, substituting at once some thought of me for the fear.

The powers of evil watch you as a besieging force would watch a guarded city—the object being always to find some weak spot, attack that, and so gain an entrance. So evil lurks around you, and seeks to surprise you in some fear.

The fear may have been but a small one, but it affords evil a weak spot of attack and entrance, and then in come rushing despondency, doubt of me, and so many other sins. Pray, my beloved children, for that Perfect love of me that indeed casts out all fear.

DEPRESSION   DECEMBER 20

Fight fear as you would fight a plague. Fight it in my name. . . . Fear, even the smallest fear, is the hacking at the cords of love that bind you to me.

However small the impression, in time those cords will wear thin, and then one disappointment, or shock and they snap. But for the little fears the cords of love would have held.

Fight fear.

Depression is a state of fear. Fight that too. Fight. Fight. Depression is the impression left by fear. Fight and conquer, and oh! For love of me, for the sake of my tender, never-failing love of you, fight and love and win.

SMILE INDULGENTLY   DECEMBER 21

Children, take every moment as of my Planning and ordering. Remember your master is the Lord of the day's little happenings. In all the small things yield to my gentle pressure on your arm. Stay or go, as that pressure, love's pressure, indicates.

The Lord of the moments, Creator of the snowdrop and the mighty oak. More tender with the snowdrop than the oak.

And when things do not fall out according to your plan, then smile at me indulgently, a smile of love, and say, as you would to a human loved one "Have your way then"—knowing that my loving response will be to make that way as easy for your feet as it can be.

PRACTICE PROTECTION   DECEMBER 22

Fear no evil because I have conquered evil. It has power to hurt only those who do not place themselves under my protection. This is not a question of feeling, it is an assured fact.

All you have to do is to say with assurance that whatever it is cannot harm you, as I have conquered it. Children, in not only the big, but the little things of life, be sure of my conquering power. Know that all is well. Be sure of it. Practice this. Learn it until it is unfailing and instinctive with you.

But practice it in the quite small things, and then you will find you will do it easily, naturally, lovingly, trustingly, in the big things of life.

THE WORLD'S SONG   DECEMBER 23

Bless us, O Lord, we beseech Thee and show us the way in which Thou wouldst have us walk.

Walk with me in the way of peace. Shed peace, not discord, wherever you go. But it must be my peace.

Never a peace that is a truce with the power of evil. Never harmony if that means your life-music being adapted to the mood and music of the world.

My disciples so often make the mistake of thinking all must be harmonious. No! Not when it means singing the song of the world.

I, the Prince of peace, said that I came "not to bring peace but a sword."

HE IS COMING   DECEMBER 24

Our Lord, Thou art here. Let us feel Thy nearness.

Yes! But remember the first hail must be that of the Magi in the Bethlehem stable. Not as king and Lord in heavenly triumph must you first hail me. But as amongst the lowliest, bereft of earth's pomp like the Magi.

So to the humble the worship of humility—the Bethlehem Babe—must be the first hail.

Then the worship of repentance. As earth's sinner, you stand by me in the Jordan, baptized of John, worshipping me the friend and Servant of Sinners.

Dwell much on my life. Step out beside me. Share it with me. Humility, service, worship, sacrifice, sanctification—steps in the Christian life.

BABE OF BETHLEHEM   DECEMBER 25

Kneel before the Babe of Bethlehem. Accept the truth that the kingdom of heaven is for the lowly, the simple.

Bring to me, the Christ-child, your gifts, truly the gifts of earth's wisest.

The Gold—your money.

Frankincense—the adoration of a consecrated life.

Myrrh—your sharing in my sorrows and those of the world.

"And they presented unto him gifts: gold, frankincense and myrrh."

HEALTH AND WEALTH   DECEMBER 26

Be not afraid, health and wealth are coming to you both. My wealth which is sufficiency for your needs, and for my work you long to do.

Money, as some call wealth, to hoard, to display, you know is not for my disciples.

Journey through this world simply seeking the means to do my will and work. Never keep anything you are not using. Remember all I give you will be mine, only given to you to use. Could you think of me hoarding my treasures? You must never do it. Rely on me.

To store for the future is to *fear* and to doubt me. Check every doubt of me at once. Live in the joy of my constant presence. Yield every moment to me. Perform every task, however humble, as at my gentle bidding, and for me, for love of me. So live, so love, so work.

You are the apostles of the little services.

GLORIOUS WORK   DECEMBER 27

I have stripped you of much, that it should be truly a life of well-being. Build up stone by stone upon a firm foundation, and that rock is your master—that rock is Christ.

A life of discipline and of joyous fulfillment is to be yours. . . . Never lose sight of the glorious work to which you have been called.

Let no riches, no ease entice you from the path of miracle-working with me upon which your feet are set. Love and laugh. Trust and pray. Ride on now in a loving humility to victory.

SIGNS AND FEELINGS   DECEMBER 28

Our Lord, Thou art here. Let us feel Thy nearness.

I am here. Do not need *feeling* too much. To ask for feeling too much is to ask for a sign, and then the answer is the same as that I gave when on earth. "There shall no sign be given but the sign of the prophet Jonas. . . . For as Jonas was three days and three nights . . . so shall the Son of Man be three days and three nights in the heart of the earth."

Veiled from sight to the unbeliever. To the believer the veiling is only temporary, to be followed by a glorious resurrection. . . .

What does it matter what you feel? What matters is what I am, was, and ever shall be to you—A risen Lord. . . . The *feeling* that I am with you may depend upon any passing mood of yours—upon a change of circumstances, upon a mere trifle.

I am uninfluenced by circumstances. . . . My promise given is kept. I am here, one with you in tender loving friendship.

WORK AND PRAYER   DECEMBER 29

Work and prayer represent the two forces that will ensure you success. Your work and my work.

For prayer, believing prayer, is based on the certainty that *I* am working for you and with you and in you.

Go forward gladly and unafraid. I am with you. With men your task may be impossible, but with God all things are possible.

FISHERS OF MEN   DECEMBER 30

When you think of those of whom you read who are in anguish do you ever think how my heart must ache with the woe of it, with the anguish of it?

If I beheld the city and wept over it how much more should I weep over the agony of these troubled hearts, over lives that seek to live without my sustaining power.

"They will not come unto me that they might have life."

Live to bring others to *me,* the only source of happiness and heart-peace.

JESUS THE CONQUEROR   DECEMBER 31

Jesus. That is the name by which you conquer. Jesus. Not as cringing suppliants but as those recognizing a friend, say my name—Jesus. "Thou shall call his name Jesus, for he shall save his people from their sins."

And in that word "sins" read not only vice and degradation, but doubts, fears, tempers, despondencies, impatience, lack of love in big and little things. Jesus. "He shall save his people from their sins." The very uttering of the name lifts the soul away from petty valley-irritations to mountain heights.

"He shall save his people from their sins." Savior and friend, joy-bringer and rescuer, leader and guide—Jesus. Do you need delivering from cowardice, from adverse circumstances, from poverty, from failure, from weakness?

"There is none other name . . . whereby you can be saved"—*Jesus*. Say it often. Claim the power it brings.

HOLY LAUGHTER OF
GOD CALLING